ST. LOUIS POST-DISPATCH

YADI

THE LEGENDARY CAREER OF YADIER MOLINA

Library of Congress Cataloguing-in-Publication Data available upon request

This book is available in quantity at special discounts for your group or organization. For further information, contact:

Triumph Books LLC
814 North Franklin Street
Chicago, Illinois 60610
(312) 337-0747
www.triumphbooks.com

Printed in U.S.A.
ISBN: 978-1-63727-100-1

ST. LOUIS POST-DISPATCH

Roger Hensley, Sports Editor
Gary Hairlson, Multimedia Director

Design and page production by Patricia Frey
Cover design by Preston Pisellini

CREDITS AND ACKNOWLEDGMENTS

ST. LOUIS POST-DISPATCH PHOTOGRAPHS BY David Carson, 3, 69, 71, 116, 121, 137, 139, 141; Robert Cohen, 1, 40–41, 94–95, 133, 135, 144; J.B. Forbes, 73; Christian Gooden, 104, 113, 115, 119; Chris Lee, 8-9, 11, 12, 15, 16, 19, 21, 23, 25, 29, 32, 43, 54, 60, 65 (bottom), 67, 75–77, 83, 89, 90, 122; Huy Richard Mach, 84; Laurie Skrivan, 96, 101, 109, 125, 126, 130

ADDITIONAL PHOTOGRAPHS COURTESY OF AP/Wide World Photos, 107 (Gregory Bull); 111 (Tom Gannam); 45, 63 (Charles Krupa); 27 (David J. Phillip); 51, 57 (Jeff Robertson); 66, 87 (Matt Slocum); 37, 38 (Tom Uhlman); Getty Images, 65 (top), (Streeter Lecka); Courtesy of Evelyn Guadalupe and Fundacion 4, 79, 81; Courtesy of Yadier Molina's Instagram page, 93

CONTENTS

INTRODUCTION

'The mainstay': Yadier Molina outwitted, outworked opponents in legendary Cardinals career

By Derrick Goold
September 29, 2022

One word was all Cardinals manager Oliver Marmol wanted to hear from each player he asked, one word that would say a lot and, upon detailed inspection, reveal so much more.

In his first spring training at the helm, Marmol asked several players how they, personally, would want their offense to be described at season's end. He did not want a sentence or dissertation. He requested one word, a brief description that might lead to further conversation. He fielded the familiar adjectives. Tough. Relentless. And then Yadier Molina answered.

"Smart."

Born into a baseball family and bronzed as a champion in a baseball city, Molina spent his career steps ahead of the stats — excelling at pitch-framing before it was pixelated, shutting down running games faster than analytics could. He molded games in ways box scores still haven't captured. Instead of the usual cacophony of numbers to describe an elite player, peers and coaches search for synonyms for how Molina intuitively sways the game. They note his "baseball IQ," call him "the most intelligent player on the field," and say he "uses a different set of lenses." His brother, former big-leaguer Bengie Molina, said "he sees the sixth inning while you're playing the third."

Yadier's game is a 3-D stereogram — a vibrant picture, but relax the eyes and new depth appears.

Thrust into Puerto Rico's Coliceba league at 15 and playing against strong amateurs, some twice his age, Molina studied the edges, how seasoned players sprang hidden ball tricks, and he learned to level the playing field. He was gifted with eye-hand coordination for contact at the plate and stealing strikes behind it. But he wasn't going to be the biggest or strongest or fastest on the field. He would not outslug or outrun opponents, so he found another way to outplay them. In one word: outsmart.

"People have some doubt, because obviously you don't run, you don't have power. What can you do?" Molina told the Post-Dispatch. "So, I put that in my mind. I was like, 'One day I'm going to prove you wrong.' And I think I did. I think I did.

"I love everything about baseball because you have to think about baseball," he continued. "You have to think about what you're going to do. You have to think about what you did last week against those guys. You have to think about what you're going to do next week, tomorrow, today. That's part of my game. Pay attention to the little details and try to take advantage."

The last to wear No. 4 for the Cardinals, Molina will retire ranked first in categories that define a catcher's durability and, considering the demands of the position, illustrate he's one of the most influential players of his generation. His 19 seasons with the Cardinals are second to Stan Musial's 22, his nine Gold Glove awards second to Ozzie Smith as a Cardinal and behind Ivan Rodriguez and Johnny Bench at catcher. No player has more putouts — more than 5,013 innings worth of them. Opponents just stopped running on Molina: The 1,358 steal attempts against the Cardinals since 2005 are the fewest by 500. Twenty-seven teams have allowed more steals than opponents have even tried against the Cardinals.

Molina's the only catcher with 2,200 games for one team and one of four full-time catchers with at least 2,000 hits. No National League catcher has a better career winning percentage (.560) or more shutouts (157), and no NL player has appeared in more postseason games (102, so far). Molina called the curveball that froze Carlos Beltran and hit the homer in that 2006 game that clinched the pennant. David Freese headlined the 2011 World Series drama, but Molina had more RBIs in it, nine to seven. The two seasons immediately after Albert Pujols left for the Angels, Molina finished fourth and third in MVP voting.

The sum of it all is "he strictly wants to win," said Marmol.

Since Molina's debut in June 2004, the Cardinals have played more than 2,920 regular-season games. They have been mathematically out of contention from the playoffs in 24.

Total.

"Yadi has been the mainstay — always there, always back there, always leading them," former MVP Christian Yelich said. "Sometimes it feels like he knows what you're thinking."

"I think Yadi has been the staple, one of the better catchers, if not the best catcher, for as long as I've been in baseball," said Cubs manager and former catcher David Ross.

"Yadi's been a quiet type," said Atlanta third base coach Ron Washington, Texas' manager in the 2011 World Series loss to the Cardinals. "He just does most

of what he does with his actions. Whatever you do decide to do you better be 100% right because he's back there thinking how he can be 100% right to shut you down. He doesn't miss anything on the field. That's what tremendous catchers and Hall of Fame catchers do. You definitely have to change your game plan because of his intelligence behind the plate."

OUTWIT, OUTWORK, OUTPLAY

Head home with Molina after a game for a sense of how he ingests a kaleidoscopic amount of baseball and finds the patterns. At any time, he may have three or four games on TVs at once, and sometimes he'll have YouTube playing a game 20, 30 years old. He will know the outcome and still groan or holler when he spots a poor pitch sequence or mistake, friends describe.

He will suggest a hit and run in one game — and call it before it happens in another.

"Like a religion in my family," Molina explained. "That's why I play."

Bench told Wainwright that Molina was the best defensive catcher he's ever seen. Once asked what Molina does that other catchers should borrow, Buster Posey, a contemporary and former MVP, answered: "Everything." Sandy Alomar Jr., whose play Molina mimicked as a young catcher, turned to the martial arts for a comparison of Molina. Like Bruce Lee, Alomar said, Molina invented his own style. When Houston catcher Christian Vazquez became the starter for the Red Sox, he texted Molina for advice: "How do you get better as a leader, so that your teammates respect you more?"

Lead by work was the reply.

"I feel like my era, whenever someone was, 'Oh you want to be a catcher?' The answer is, 'Oh, yeah, I want to be like Yadier Molina,'" said Yankees All-Star catcher Jose Trevino, who wears his hat backward under his mask to be like Yadier Molina. "It's the same thing as kids who want to be a shortstop want to be like Derek Jeter."

Players often talk about the greats with amazement.

Peers talk about Molina with reverence.

"I've said this to my closest friends and other dads," former teammate Matt Carpenter said. "There is just an extra layer to the Hall of Fame player — of toughness, of grit, of knowledge. Real students of the game. The aptitude of the game. And competitiveness. Yadi embodies all of that. You hear it all the time about the greats like Michael Jordan, Kobe Bryant — they make everyone else around them better. Yadi does, for sure."

QUICK STUDY

The Cardinals selected the youngest of the Molina boys in the fourth round of the 2000 draft and sent scout Steve Turco to evaluate him at an American Legion tournament and determine if Molina was worth a higher bonus.

President of baseball operations John Mozeliak, the director of scouting at the time, recalled his exchange with Turco.

"What did you think of Yadier Molina when you saw him?"

"Give him whatever he wants."

Molina's two brothers, Bengie and Jose, had already been in the majors, and he was the well-known son of a Hall of Fame amateur infielder, Benjamin Molina. Benjamin spent so much time coaching baseball and tending to the ballpark that kids knew him as El Senor que Los Campos, the caretaker of the field. The Molinas lived in Vega Alta, Puerto Rico, an area known as El Pueblo de los Nangotoas, or Village of the Squatters. The nickname comes from the pose workers had waiting for the train. Molina once said he knew baseball was his way up and out.

Before the draft, Molina attended a workout in Cincinnati and left convinced the House of Bench was going to draft him, and high. He never forgot how the Reds passed and sought the same bonus. On Turco's advice, the Cardinals signed him for $325,000.

Molina reported to instructional league and, as he later described, knew how to win, knew the game, had a good arm, "but didn't know much about catching skills." Then he met the man he called "my angel" — beloved coach Dave Ricketts. A demanding and devoted mentor, Ricketts once pulled Molina out of a game for a rigorous series of blocking-ball drills and then returned him to the game. When the Cardinals canvassed their coaches for suggestions who could catch Rick Ankiel as he battled wildness and doubt, Ricketts said Molina could.

He was 18. Word was getting around.

"You dig a little deeper for the moments he takes over because they don't stand out like watching Albert Pujols hit the ball off the Big Mac sign," former starter Chris Carpenter said. "It really all goes back to how much he cares. His care factor of really wanting to invest himself into his career, into the game of baseball was really big. He cared about knowing, he cared about paying attention, he cared about what was going on around him, and he cared about your success. He cared about what he could give teammates. He cared about preparation. He cared about his failures. He showed up to the ballpark every day trying to understand something more."

In a Chris Carpenter start at Pittsburgh in May 2010, Molina chased a runner back to third base, where another Pirate was already standing. Molina knew the rule — but tagged the runner who was safe. When that Bucco left the base, Molina tagged him again for the double play to end the inning. The Cardinals won, 4-3. Molina had four hits.

This season, Molina caught sight of how the Giants were relaying signs to runners, and, in the middle of an at-bat, decoded a hit-and-run. He called for a pitch out and easily threw a runner out to end the inning. In 2017, the Reds drew a two-out walk to load the bases, and Molina stood casually at home as if surveying the mess. He was waiting for what he spied a runner do weeks earlier. Eugenio Suarez strolled into third and then a step past it. Molina whipped the ball to Jedd Gyorko for an out that ended the inning. Molina will position the defense so the hitter thinks he knows the pitcher is coming inside and then, as coaches wince in the dugout, call an outside pitch.

"I'm always going to be fascinated by Yadier Molina because I've seen all of his tricks, and I know he has more in there," former teammate Kolten Wong said.

"I think we've all learned from watching him play," Milwaukee manager Craig Counsell said. "What's always the most impressive is how he … feels the game. He's got this innate sense of what's going to happen in the game and that's really powerful. He's as good at it as anybody."

TRICKS OF THE TRADE

In the midst of a record-setting 17-game winning streak and at the start of the heated fantasy football season, Wainwright stood on the mound, trouble percolating all around him.

Out walked his trusted confidant, his compass, his catcher.

"You want Hill?" Molina said. "Alright, Hill?"

Hill was wide receiver Tyreek Hill, a fantasy juggernaut for Kansas City, and for weeks Wainwright had been trying to lure Molina into a trade. Wainwright's team needed a star, Molina's needed depth. And now Molina needed a distraction.

"We start going over trade scenarios in the middle of the game," Wainwright said. "OK, alright, no, I'm not doing that. It has to be a fair trade. And all of sudden the game wasn't speeding up on me anymore, slowed down, and I was able to go out and pitch."

Ask four pitchers about Molina's manner on the mound, and they're likely to describe four different Molinas. He reads them and what they need like he reads hitters. He never talked fantasy football with Chris Carpenter. At least two pitchers, John Lackey and Mitchell Boggs, shook off Molina's calls so often that he just waved them on. Throw whatever they want. He'd figure it out. No signs.

"He's catching 94-96 mph with good run and a hammer for a breaking ball — and he's framing it with no idea what was coming," former teammate Matt Holliday said.

They stopped shaking him off.

When Edward Mujica arrived for his first day with the Cardinals after a trade, he tracked down a coach to ask for a scouting report. The coach delivered it: "Follow Yadi."

The commitment Molina inspires in teammates explains one of his nicknames in Puerto Rico: "El Lider." He earned it as the heart and engine of Team Puerto Rico during its captivating run in the 2017 World Baseball Classic — a run that included Molina catching an opponent off first base as he celebrated a single. The nickname took on deeper meaning when Molina gathered necessities and personally delivered them to areas devastated by Hurricane Maria.

"More than a nickname — it means he's the leader of all leaders," said Cardinals broadcaster Polo Ascensio.

The Wainwrights visited the Molinas in Puerto Rico for Thanksgiving dinner in 2021, and as the recognizable right-hander played a nearby golf course, one worker greeted him.

"He said, 'Thank you for coming and visiting the great Yadier Molina,'" Wainwright recalled. "'We know about you, and we know you're a Christian. And you have your Jesus. And we have our Yadier Molina.'"

So have the Cardinals, for 19 seasons.

When Mark McGwire returned to be hitting coach in 2010, then manager Tony La Russa confessed that the Cardinals had a dilemma — the essential player could soon leave as a free agent. Not Pujols, McGwire recalled later: "Yadi." Molina remained for another dozen seasons, winning two of the four NL pennants in his era and closing his career as a part of 15 consecutive winning teams. It took a dozen years, but the Cardinals, like their catcher, saw this coming.

Contributions beyond the most advanced stats will now be revealed — a presence finally measured by the absence it leaves.

"What's that look like?" bench coach and longtime teammate Skip Schumaker said. "I don't know where this organization would be without Yadi. For almost 20 years we got to watch him. He made us better for years to come. Here's where I am: Maybe we shouldn't think of what it's like when he's gone, but be thankful we were here for what he did for so long." ∎

The Cardinals' Yadier Molina is mobbed by teammates David Eckstein, Randy Flores and Ryan Ludwick after his game-winning single in the 10th inning Wednesday, Sept. 19, 2007.

2004 – 2010

The ability of Yadier Molina to throw out runners caught elder brother Jose's attention.

YADIER IS THE LATEST MOLINA TO CATCH ON IN THE BIG LEAGUES

By Dirk Chatelain
August 13, 2004

It was summer in Puerto Rico and that meant baseball on every street. Suntanned teens rolled out of bed and skipped breakfast and poured out of screen doors, stopping only to slide a hand into an old glove.

They divided into teams of 10 or 12. They skipped lunch and used paper for bases and played inning after inning, stopping only at the sound of a mother's voice.

"Car coming!" yelled the mother of a boy named Yadi. "Watch out for the car!"

Gladys Molina had three boys on that street in Vega Alta. Years later, they all went on to play major league baseball thousands of miles away.

Bengie was the oldest; Jose a year younger. They're now catching for the Anaheim Angels. Yadier, a rookie with the Cardinals, was seven years younger. The brothers called him a baby. They said he couldn't play. He did anyway. Since the day he was born, Jose said, Yadi had a bat in his hand.

"Sometimes we didn't eat to play baseball," Yadier Molina said. "Go home, go to sleep, get up the next morning and do it again."

Like most kids in Puerto Rico, Yadi wanted to be a catcher. Ivan Rodriguez — "Pudge" to the kids in Vega Alta — grew up 10 miles from the Molinas' street. Sandy Alomar was from Puerto Rico. So was Jorge Posada and Javy Lopez and Benito Santiago.

"You saw those guys in the papers every day," Jose Molina said. "You looked up to them."

The chest protector hung down to Yadi's knees the first time he wore it. He played the position full time after he turned 15, even when a thrown bat hit him in the chest or a ball bounced off the pavement into his lip. "Any blood?" they asked. Even if there was — they played on.

"To me, the difference between the Americans and us is we want the hard job," said Molina, 22, whose father played professionally and was recently inducted into the Puerto Rico Superior Baseball League Hall of Fame. "Basically, because we've got so many catchers in the major leagues. We like to be dirty."

By the time scouts heard about the third Molina, Bengie and Jose were in America playing professionally. Yadi was well on his way to joining them. Jose knew it when he came home in the winter and watched his little brother gun down runners at second base, or when Yadi blocked a ball in the dirt that should've been a wild pitch.

The youngest Molina was drafted when he was 17. He moved through the St. Louis farm system and started the 2004 season in Triple-A. He expected to stay there for a while. But a Mike Matheny injury meant a phone call and a promotion on June 3. He hasn't been sent back.

He says he is "lucky" to be a Cardinal in a pennant race. Those who wear the same uniform disagree.

"I don't know if I've played with anybody who's been that young that does what he does on this level," 11-year veteran pitcher Cal Eldred said. "Bottom line."

"Some guys come up and rub guys the wrong way, but he's here early and he's the last one to leave," said Ray King, whose locker is next to Molina's in the Cardinals clubhouse. "And that's what you like to see from a rookie."

The Cards' likely catcher of the future, who is hitting .253 in 91 at-bats, is quiet in the clubhouse.

BETTER LATE THAN NEVER?

By Joe Strauss

OCTOBER 28, 2004 — After considering the switch for Game 3, La Russa returned second baseman Tony Womack to the leadoff spot Wednesday night while replacing Reggie Sanders with John Mabry in left field and Mike Matheny with rookie Yadier Molina behind the plate. Womack responded by leading off the Cardinals' first with a single, which turned out to be his team's only hit through four innings.

Mabry's start was his second of the postseason, the same as Molina.

"John, when he started, gave us another option, whether it was left, third or first base," La Russa said. "So we're looking for that tonight."

Sanders sat after enduring nine hitless at-bats with five strikeouts through three games, dropping his postseason average to .182. Matheny was hitting .250 for the Series and .195 for the postseason; Molina also caught Marquis in his Game 4 start in the NLCS against the Houston Astros.

"If we win this game tonight, Mike will be fresh for tomorrow," La Russa said.

Cardinals catcher Yadier Molina passes third base coach Jose Oquendo enroute to scoring in the second inning on a single by Albert Pujols during a game between the St. Louis Cardinals and the Oakland Athletics at Busch Stadium in St. Louis, Mo. on June 15, 2004.

But under the lights, he's got a slingshot for an arm. He's not afraid to call the breaking ball with a runner at third in a tie game. He wants it in the dirt.

He's not afraid to go to the mound, look Jason Isringhausen in the eye and give him a tip. He knows Izzy will listen.

He's not afraid to go to the plate with two out, the bases loaded and the game tied in the bottom of the ninth inning. That was last Saturday against the Mets. Molina got the game-winning hit.

"You don't have to be afraid in this game," said Molina, who talks to his brothers about twice a week, receiving advice on hitters and pitchers.

"No, you just have to play the game hard. Respect the game. Respect everybody and everybody's going to respect you. The way I see it is you have to go out and play the game the right way.

"I'm a rookie but I know what it's about."

He also knows there are kids in Vega Alta playing on the streets right now. It's the 25th inning of their game and the sun is beating down and they've got no plans to go home any time soon. They know about Pudge and they know about Javy and Jorge. And they're hearing more and more about Yadi.

Said Molina: "I just wanted to be one more." ∎

Catcher Yadier Molina's poise under fire has impressed the Cardinals' pitching staff.

IN YADI THEY TRUST

Molina is ready to be everyday catcher at 22, Cards say

By Derrick Goold
March 3, 2005

JUPITER, Fla. — The only thing that whizzed through the Cardinals' minor-league system quicker than Yadier Molina in the past four years was word on how good this catching prodigy with rich pedigree was going to be.

As if Molina being preceded to the majors by two brothers wasn't enough, the reports that heralded his eventual arrival as the Cardinals' starting catcher were lustrous.

Eventual is now imminent.

"For me, when you hear people talk about him — and you've got (scouts) you trust and you hear what they are saying — you develop a certain opinion about him," Cardinals pitching coach Dave Duncan said. "Our expectations were very high for Yadi before we ever saw him play. ... During the championship season, he played as if he's played in the big leagues for many years, as if he was experienced.

"He's a very smart kid with great instincts for the game."

Molina will start the Cardinals' Grapefruit League opener tonight — in Port St. Lucie, Fla., against the New York Mets — as the team's everyday catcher, replacing his mentor, Mike Matheny.

It signals officially what happened in Game 4 of the World Series. Molina started then in place of Matheny, who signed in the offseason with San Francisco.

"Every day, I watched what he did," Molina said, looking back on his season of apprenticing with the Gold Glove catcher. "We talked about hitters, every day. We did the same (routine), everyday. ... I was a rookie. I just wanted to be quiet, listen. This year, I'm going to be more comfortable to do more."

Through the spring workouts, Molina has been affixed to the Cardinals' starters, including Rick Ankiel in his best outing of spring, and several relievers. As games begin tonight with him working with new ace Mark Mulder, much of his game time will be tied to starters' game time.

At 22, Molina will be the youngest everyday catcher in the National League, and he inherits a staff that finished one run shy of winning the ERA title. Only five teams in baseball have started a catcher 22 or younger and made it to the World Series, though the Cardinals have done it three times.

The Cardinals say Molina's age only makes his catchers' sense more remarkable. Consider how quickly Molina — a native of Puerto Rico, younger brother of both Angels catchers — won the staff's trust.

"Confidence is a lot of it," pitcher Matt Morris said. "Yadi has been — well, everybody was really impressed with his talent and saw how good he was going to be. At the start, he won us all over with his poise. He keeps his head cool in heated situations, in tough situations. Pitchers want to lean on that type of catcher."

Six days after making his debut he instinctively intercepted Chicago's Derrek Lee on the first baseman's way to confront Morris about a chin-buzzing pitch. The benches emptied, but Molina was even-keeled. Or, how about the gridiron shot he took from Ty Wigginton in Pittsburgh? A vicious collision at the plate that Molina won by holding Larry Walker's throw and tagging Wigginton out. Two weeks earlier, Wigginton had plowed into a catcher in a similar spot and broke the catcher's ankle.

And scored the run.

In the third inning of his first World Series game, Molina stood up from behind the plate to confront the batter coming forward — eventual series MVP Manny Ramirez. They spoke in Spanish, Molina succinctly telling Ramirez that he felt David Ortiz was barking out pitch location from the on-deck circle. It was a warning. Ramirez denies Ortiz was doing anything. Molina continues to decline to discuss details.

"You have to do what you have to," he said. "No big deal."

But it is part of the bigger picture.

His hitting continues to improve; he finished 10th in batting in Puerto Rico's winter league. He was dubbed defensively ready for the bigs when he was in Class A in 2002. (He threw out 50 percent of attempted thefts last season.) What he got from Matheny was the vet's contagious curiosity and studiousness. Molina had not watched video before joining Matheny, and is now a scouting junkie. He spoke little in pitching staff meetings. But when he did, it caught people's attention.

"He doesn't talk a lot, but when he does it makes a lot of sense," said Duncan, who will let Molina call pitches, call games just as Matheny did. "That tends to gain respect."

As does his buoyant nature. Manager Tony La Russa said he's got a "great smile."

Roger Cedeno gushed about Molina's "good heart."

Players laud how inquisitive he is, firing a question and soaking in the answer.

"He's a young guy who has his ears open all the time, always willing to learn whether it's from us, from the pitching coach, from the manager, from another position player," said Jason Marquis, who threw mostly to Molina. Marquis won seven of his first nine outings with Molina, and in 15 games together Marquis' ERA was 3.57. "He wants to do what it takes. He's willing to take any angle to get that edge. That's what makes him special." ■

The Cards' Yadier Molina, who was a rookie last season, said: "This year, I'm going to be more comfortable to do more."

AMAZIN'

YADI'S DRIVE SENDS CARDS TO MOTOWN

Suppan holds Mets in check

By Joe Strauss
October 20, 2006

NEW YORK — The ball kept climbing, then hanging and, finally, it fell.

And when it landed a dozen or so feet beyond Shea Stadium's left-field wall with one out in Thursday night's ninth inning, Yadier Molina's six months of struggle magically transformed into an indelible marker within an increasingly improbable season.

Molina, a precocious defensive talent often left to feel self-conscious about his hitting, shoved the Cardinals into their 17th World Series by turning New York Mets righthanded reliever Aaron Heilman's breaking ball into a two-run home run. The blast snapped a 1-1 Game 7 tie and gave the Cardinals a 3-1 lead that nervous rookie closer Adam Wainwright clung to for the franchise's second pennant in three years.

"It stayed there a long time. I didn't know where it was coming down," Molina said. "When it came down, I just looked into my dugout and saw everybody jumping up and down screaming. It's the best feeling I've ever had."

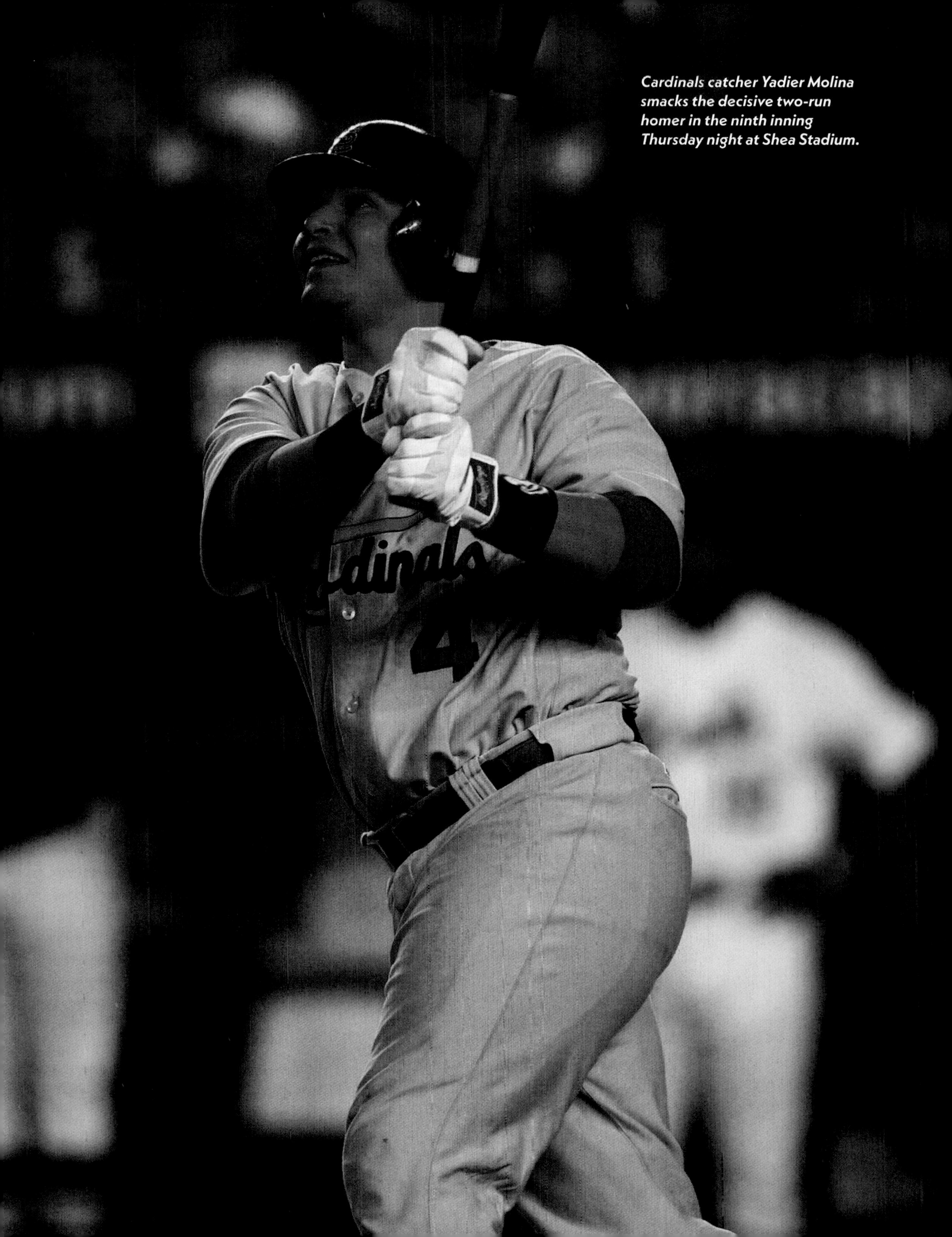

Cardinals catcher Yadier Molina smacks the decisive two-run homer in the ninth inning Thursday night at Shea Stadium.

Wainwright survived consecutive singles to begin the ninth and a bases-loading two-out walk by striking out Cardinals nemesis Carlos Beltran on three straight pitches. The third, a sharp-breaking curve, froze Beltran for a called strike three.

"I'm not a guy who gets nervous. I can remember only a handful of times in my life when I've been really nervous. This was the most nervous I've ever been in my life," Wainwright said.

Only 24, Molina sped to the major leagues in only 1,044 minor-league at-bats. Among his teammates, only Albert Pujols got there more quickly. Molina struggled to a .216 average while becoming a man of 1,000 stances this season. Only upon reaching the postseason has he found a comfort zone that brought him a .333 average with two home runs, a team-high seven RBIs and the most telling swing of a riveting October.

"I just prayed," Molina said. "I prayed Endy Chavez wouldn't catch the ball."

Chavez, the Mets' left fielder, had denied the Cardinals a 3-1 lead in the sixth inning when he reached over the same wall to steal a two-run homer from Scott Rolen.

"That's a better swing than I've had in the past two postseasons," said Rolen, who hit the game-winning home run of the 2004 NLCS against Houston Astros ace Roger Clemens.

Against Molina, however, Chavez could only retreat, look up and stare at an advertising slogan proclaiming "The Strength To Be There."

An 83-win team that played less than .500 ball for the season's final five months equaled a major league record for the fewest wins by a team advancing to the World Series.

A team that took two weeks to win its final four regular-season games stands four victories away from its first World Series championship since 1982. All they need to do is go through the 95-win Detroit Tigers.

Molina's lightning bolt against a drizzly Queens night stunned a crowd of 56,357 but didn't come in time to make a winning pitcher of series MVP Jeff

Suppan for his seven-plus innings of two-hit ball. It didn't have to. Suppan already had established himself as an October rock by starting the Cardinals' third clinching victory in three years.

"I never thought I'd be in a situation like this," said Suppan, who has risen from an "innings eater" to a certified big-game pitcher in three years with this current team.

Lefthander Randy Flores took the most significant decision of his career in return for two eighth-inning strikeouts and a ground ball.

"The best moment possible, winning Game 7 of the NLCS," he said, "unless you're talking about Game 7 of the World Series."

A pitching staff that slogged its way to a 4.54 ERA one year after leading the major leagues in the same category snuffed the Mets' powerful lineup with a 3.84 ERA. Rookies finished five of the seven games, including all the wins.

"People will never know all the stuff this team has been through — some of it but not all of it," remarked pitching coach Dave Duncan. "This has been an extremely difficult year in a lot of ways. But I really thought coming into this series we had a chance if we executed really well and we scored some runs. It's a credit to these pitchers. They did a very good job start to finish."

The Cardinals tied the 1973 Mets for carrying the fewest regular-season wins to the World Series. Whichever manager, Tony La Russa or Detroit's Jim Leyland, wins the title, he will join Sparky Anderson as the only managers in the game's history to win World Series championships in both leagues.

For La Russa, who previously won with the dynastic 1989 Oakland A's, this ride is something more unexpected and, in a way, redemptive. La Russa has long carried Charlie Lau's definition of "a good team" with him. The famed hitting coach once told La Russa a team can't be considered good unless it wins 90 games.

"I thought about it in the car coming down here today," the manager said. "This was 90 wins. Now we can call ourselves a good team."

Yadier Molina rounds the bases after hitting the game-winning, two-run homer in the ninth inning Thursday night.

"Oh, we've had better teams," said center fielder Jim Edmonds. "This is not the best team we've had. We've had much better teams. But I don't think we've had a team that's battled and battled like this one. This team may be the one that's best at battling through that I've been on. And we did it when nobody thought we could do it."

Suppan, a guy who reached the Cardinals via free agency three Decembers ago as a 62-75 pitcher, dueled for six innings with enigmatic lefthander Oliver Perez, a Pittsburgh Pirates castoff deemed too excitable and too much an injury risk to ever match his sizable potential.

The Mets reached him for a 1-0 lead with two outs in the first inning.

Beltran beat left fielder Preston Wilson's throw for a two-out double. Suppan then walked cleanup hitter Carlos Delgado for the first of three times before third baseman David Wright flared a single short of right fielder Juan Encarnacion.

The Cardinals' first chance came after Edmonds led off the second inning with a single. Advanced to third base by Molina's parachute single to left, Edmonds was in position to score when No. 8 hitter Ronnie Belliard perfectly executed a safety squeeze on a high fastball.

There the game froze as Suppan didn't allow another hit before being lifted in the eighth inning.

The Mets loaded the bases with one out in the sixth when Delgado walked, Rolen threw wildly into the first-base stands on Wright's ground ball and right fielder Shawn Green was walked intentionally.

Adopting a soft, softer, softest approach, Suppan struck out second baseman Jose Valentin as his velocity decelerated through the at-bat. Chavez, poised to join New York's line of October icons, instead ended the threat with a fly ball to center field.

Thursday's performance left Suppan with one run allowed in 15 innings this series. In five NLCS starts for the Cardinals, Suppan has allowed six earned runs in 32 innings for a 1.69 ERA. ∎

MOLINA SIGNS FOUR-YEAR DEAL

Cards avoid going to arbitration with 'a cornerstone of this club'

By Derrick Goold
January 22, 2008

After several seasons of lauding their young catcher as a pillar of the team, the Cardinals put a contract where their compliments have been.

The Cardinals signed Yadier Molina to a four-year, $15.5 million deal that certifies his importance even as it cements a new member of the club's younger core.

"He's definitely a cornerstone of this club moving forward," general manager John Mozeliak said Monday at the news conference to announce the deal. "If we didn't feel he had those capabilities (as a leader), or hadn't exhibited them to this point, we probably wouldn't even be talking of this type of deal. The reality is, it's really a compliment of what he's done and our assumption is it will continue."

The contract extends through 2011 and includes a $7 million team option for 2012. The deal keeps the parties out of an arbitration hearing, offers Molina multiple-year security and buys the catcher out of at least one year of free agency.

The Cardinals chose the annual Winter Warm-up as the forum to announce the contract, and a parade of teammates that followed Molina into the media room lauded the catcher's ability and presence. Over the weekend, ace Chris Carpenter said the absence of Scott Rolen, Jim Edmonds and David Eckstein only opened the way for a player like Molina to assert his role in the clubhouse.

A multiple-year deal adds gravity to Molina's authority.

Not that he needed it, manager Tony La Russa said.

"I'm one of the guys who doesn't get afraid of anything," Molina said Monday. "If I have to say something to anybody, I do it. I would like to do it. We've got a young team this year, so they will need some experience. I only have three years ... but I love to (lead)."

Molina became the Cardinals' everyday starter at catcher in 2005. In three seasons, he's already established himself as one of the elite defensive players in the game. Molina threw out more would-be base stealers (27) than he allowed (23) last season. So dominant is his throwing arm that several opposing teams have stopped running on Molina entirely.

Despite a campaign by La Russa and favorable votes from within the division, Molina did not win a Gold Glove this past season. (Los Angeles Dodgers' catcher Russell Martin did.) Pujols said it remains Molina's chief goal.

As gifted as he is defensively, Molina continues to define himself offensively. He hit a career-best .275 in 2007, up from .216 in 2006. Once a hitter quick to ditch a stance at the plate, Molina has settled into a position and found strength in his ability to make contact.

"Last year was pretty good," he said. "It can be better."

Molina's agent and the Cardinals exchanged salaries last week for the arbitration hearing, with the team offering $1.85 million and Molina's camp requesting $2.75 million. Molina made $525,000 last season, and his new contract will pay him $2 million in 2008.

The deal covers Molina's two more years of eligibility for arbitration and, barring a $750,000 buyout of the option, two years of free agency.

Only Carpenter has a deal into 2012.

"Yadi wanted to get something done that was several years, and he wanted that to be here," said Molina's agent, Melvin Roman." ■

Man behind the mask: Yadier Molina's new deal rewards his increased production at the plate last season and his steady play behind it.

MOLINA'S 'D' HONORED IN 'WORST' YEAR

By Rick Hummel
November 7, 2008

That Cardinals catcher Yadier Molina was named winner of his first Rawlings Gold Glove on Wednesday was not a surprise to Cardinals manager Tony La Russa, who has watched Molina's progress in the majors since 2003. But it did come as something of an upset to Molina, who got the news from his agent in Puerto Rico.

"I didn't have my best season defensively," said Molina by telephone Thursday. "Sometimes you get what you should have received from two years ago."

In 2006, Molina had a fielding percentage of .995 and committed five errors. He had twice as many errors in 2008 and his fielding percentage was just ninth among National League catchers.

Not only did Molina feel he didn't have his best season defensively, he went so far as to call it his "worst."

"My percentage (32 percent) of throwing out runners was low and I committed 10 errors," he said. "That's not a good season for me. Next year, I have to go out there and put up a better season.

"Every game I try to be perfect. I don't want to commit any errors. I want to throw everybody out."

Molina did have one defensive statistic going for him in 2008. He picked off seven runners at first base, giving him 26 for his career. "That's one of my weapons," he said.

Though a little dinged up at the end of last season due to a couple of home-plate collisions, Molina expects himself to be ready for spring training in February and is hopeful of playing for his native Puerto Rico again in the second World Baseball Classic.

"(Cardinals coach) Jose Oquendo is going to be the manager and if he would pick me, I want to be proud," Molina said.

But, if anything, Puerto Rico is the cradle of catchers. Not only are there the three Molinas (Bengie, Jose and Yadier) but longtime All-Stars Pudge Rodriguez and Jorge Posada and Chicago Cubs standout Geovany Soto, who no doubt will be voted National League Rookie of the Year next week.

"Maybe," said Molina, laughing, "I'll be the bullpen catcher." ∎

CATCHY TITLE: ALL-STAR

Yadier Molina has a new label, to go with World Series champ and Gold Glover, and it befits his craft

By Joe Strauss
July 10, 2009

MILWAUKEE — Next Tuesday's All-Star Game represents an honor for Yadier Molina. It also confirms his evolution as a professional.

There has always been The Arm, the unconcealed weapon Molina has brandished since his June 2004 major-league debut to terrorize baserunners far more than they can bother him.

The Arm became Molina's reputation, but it is only a fraction of his story.

Before reaching the major leagues as Mike Matheny's heir at 21, Molina labored to follow his older brothers Bengie and Jose to this stage. Bengie won two Gold Gloves. Both brothers played for the 2002 Anaheim Angels during their world championship run. Molina was then at Peoria, struggling with the footwork and blocking fundamentals necessary to become a craftsman.

"Ever since I've been in the minor leagues, I've tried to make myself a better player. It hasn't always been easy," says Molina. "It's not supposed to be easy."

Yadier Molina has taken his batting average from a low of .216, in 2006, to the lofty plateau of .304 that he achieved last season.

> ## "He wanted to be recognized as more than just a good catcher. He wanted to be recognized as a more complete player. With the work he's put in, he has made that happen."
>
> ### —Jose Oquendo

Molina, who turns 27 Monday, already has seen much in a rich but short career. He is one of just three catchers to appear in two World Series before turning 25. The other two, Yogi Berra and Johnny Bench, are Hall of Famers. Molina reached the major leagues after taking only 1,044 minor-league at-bats. He replaced a catcher recognized as perhaps the game's best technician behind the plate. Yadier will become the first of the catching Molinas to make the All-Star Game. Bengie turns 35 this month; Jose is 34.

"He's experienced a great deal in a short period of time," says third-base coach Jose Oquendo. "He is still a young player. He's been in the World Series. He's got a Gold Glove. Now he's an All-Star. That's a lot. He deserves it. It might seem like it's taken awhile to him. But that's quick."

There has been success but also plenty of frustration along the way.

"He's had to make himself better. He struggled with things when he was younger. But to his credit Yadi has never become satisfied," says Oquendo.

Matheny and longtime minor-league instructor Dave Ricketts tutored Molina. Now perceived by many as a natural, Molina at times wept in frustration as he learned the ballet.

When Molina hit .216 in 2006, he promised that he would become an offensive presence. Two years later, Molina fulfilled his close friend Albert Pujols' prediction that he would one day hit .300 for a full major-league season.

Challenged to improve his conditioning, Molina pushed himself harder. He remains sensitive to remarks about his speed but is adept enough as a baserunner to have stolen five bases in six attempts this season.

"He wanted to be recognized as more than just a good catcher," Oquendo says. "He wanted to be recognized as a more complete player. With the work he's put in, he has made that happen."

"If you ask people, they would tell you, 'That kid works hard,'" Molina says. "I have to concentrate on working hard. I have God-given ability, but that's not enough. You have to work hard to stay here. The game is easier when you work. If you don't work, this game becomes very difficult. It will catch up to you."

Manager Tony La Russa has long seen Molina as greater than the sum of his statistics. Even when Molina labored at the plate, La Russa noted his ability to make contact and to do more with runners on base. "He's clutch. He always has been," La Russa says. "He takes a great at-bat in big situations. It's part of what makes him a great player."

Before he batted .304 in the 2008 season, Molina was a .316 hitter in 95 postseason at-bats. His Game 7 home run to beat the New York Mets in the 2006 NLCS remains an organization touchstone.

Winning a Gold Glove last season raised Molina's visibility. He won the popular vote to start next Tuesday's game after failing to be selected for the game during seasons in which he batted .275 and .304 while playing stellar defense.

"Every time you win something it's a different feeling," Molina says. "It was a great feeling to win a Gold Glove. I feel very good about making the All-Star Game. It means people recognize you as a deserving player. I think it's something you earn. It's not something that comes easily. I'm going to the park Monday and enjoy it."

Molina will fly more than a dozen friends and family from his native Puerto Rico to St. Louis for the festival.

"It's a great thing. My brothers and I grew up in a family that loved baseball. It's something we shared. My family loves to watch the game. It's part of what is special about this," Molina says.

Molina's All-Star honor comes almost nine months after the Molina patriarch, Benjamin, collapsed and died while coaching a youth league game in his native Puerto Rico. Yadier was at the field. The elder Molina was a standout amateur player and fostered a love for the game and a sense of purpose in each son. Yadier dedicated his March performance for Team Puerto Rico in the World Baseball Classic to his father.

While Bengie recently spoke of the strong emotional pull created by Bengie's possible selection as an All-Star, Yadier holds his thoughts tighter. "Bengie is my older brother. He's the one who takes care of all of us. I look up to him a lot. That's him," says Yadier, who carries his father's name as his middle name. "It's something we all experience. But we handle things differently."

Those who know him best would attest Yadier has handled them well. ■

Catching On As A Hitter

While his renowned arm and defense have been ever-present, Yadier Molina's production at the plate has helped him to gain All-Star status.

SEASON	TEAM	G	AB	R	H	HR	RBI	AVG
2004	Cardinals	51	135	12	36	2	15	.267
2005	Cardinals	114	385	36	97	8	49	.252
2006	Cardinals	129	417	29	90	6	49	.216
2007	Cardinals	111	353	30	97	6	40	.275
2008	Cardinals	124	444	37	135	7	56	.304
2009	Cardinals	76	271	26	77	5	28	.284
Career Totals		**605**	**2,005**	**170**	**532**	**92**	**237**	**.265**

Yadier Molina (second from left) celebrates in the dugout with Jaime Garcia (center) and Felipe Lopez (right) after hitting a grand slam in the ninth inning during the season-opening game against the Reds at Great American Ball Park.

CARDS OPEN SEASON BY POUNDING REDS

Home runs by Pujols, Rasmus and Molina, strong pitching by Carpenter pace the Redbirds

By Joe Strauss
April 6, 2010

CINCINNATI — It didn't take long Monday — three hitters exactly — for spring's unofficial arrival to reverberate through Great American Ball Park.

Issuing an opening day thunderclap mixed with cannon shot, first baseman Albert Pujols turned around Cincinnati Reds starting pitcher Aaron Harang's errant fastball for a solo home run that gave the Cardinals a lead they never lost.

Pujols' two-strike swing, in his first official at-bat since he needed surgery in October to remove bone chips from his right elbow, was powerful enough to wake up a season and to silence an expectant crowd of 42,493.

CARDINALS STAND TALL AS RIVALRY WITH REDS GETS PERSONAL, THEN TURNS PHYSICAL

By Bernie Miklasz
August 11, 2010

CINCINNATI — Well, Brandon Phillips got his wish. He turned himself into the center of attention. And Phillips' bravado in directing his hate speech at the Cardinals succeeded in stimulating Reds fans, who happily gave their man a hero's standing ovation.

On a steamy night at the Great American Ball Park, the Cardinals and the Reds were roiling on the river. All of the tension and anger finally bubbled over and spilled onto the field when Phillips and Cardinals catcher Yadier Molina went jaw-to-jaw in the bottom of the first.

The only thing missing was ring announcer Michael Buffer. The benches and bullpens cleared; the foul air hanging over these proceedings did not.

During a surprisingly edgy scrum for baseball, Cardinals pitcher Chris Carpenter was pinned against the backstop, Reds pitcher Johnny Cueto turned into an Eddie Murphy film character — Karate man! — and kicked Cardinals catcher Jason LaRue in the head, and both managers were ejected.

The challenge was officially thrown down. The bad blood was on the surface. The increasingly hostile Cardinals-Reds rivalry was opened raw and wide, for all to see. There would be no going back now. This wasn't a game. It was personal.

Given all of the words, spittle and dust that flew around the place on Tuesday night to charge an already static atmosphere, I was curious to see how each of the contenders would respond. Who would remain calm and professional? Who would freak out and lose composure?

The answer: Cardinals 8, Reds 4.

Cardinals manager Tony La Russa didn't necessarily enjoy watching the contest from his office. He claimed

Cardinals catcher Yadier Molina (right) starts to get into it with Cincinnati's Brandon Phillips (left) as the Reds' Paul Janish and umpire Mark Wegner try to intervene.

that he vomited four times because his stomach was churning so violently throughout the nine innings. But La Russa was proud of the victory and paid his men a supreme compliment in an ebullient postgame clubhouse.

"I'd have to search long and hard, and I've been around a long time, but I guarantee you that was tied for first," La Russa said. "I haven't had too many games in all the years I've managed that were in this category of reaching down there deep and gutting it out and playing baseball. This was as good an exhibition of that as many that I've ever been around."

And every Cardinals fan should be saying these four words today:

Thank you, Brandon Phillips.

So in his desperate, pathetic attempt to get noticed, Phillips became the perfect foil for the Cardinals. But the lightning rod became a divining rod instead.

Catcher Yadier Molina celebrates his second-inning home run against Cincinnati on Tuesday.

Because of large-mouth Phillips, the Cardinals found something that had been missing for much of the season.

I don't even know how to explain it, really. It's difficult to define. Call it mojo. Maybe it's sharpened focus. Perhaps it's esprit de corps. I do believe the Cardinals play hard, and that they care, but at times this season you just wanted to see more urgency from them. But this much is certain: the Cardinals stood as one against Cincinnati's clown prince. The Cardinals were raging Tuesday. They were on fire.

And Phillips' attack on the Cardinals — he called them "little bitches" — disintegrated into a spectacular, epic failure for the Reds. I wonder if Phillips' teammates realize that Phillips was just what the doctor of psychiatry ordered for the Cardinals.

After Monday night's game, I thought the Phillips folderol would pass. STLtoday.com ran a question Tuesday morning: Did Phillips just win the NL Central for the Cardinals? I didn't think so. I dismissed the potential impact. And there's a lot of baseball left. This may all be forgotten in a few days.

But then on Tuesday, Phillips refused to back down from his name-calling. His manager, Dusty Baker, offered a half-hearted expression of disapproval over Phillips' actions. But Baker didn't get his guy under control. And then — in an act of transparent phoniness — Phillips tapped Molina on the shin guards in a traditional baseball greeting, as if they were buddies or something.

Molina essentially told Phillips: You don't talk bad about my team like that, and then come up here and act like everything is OK.

The Cardinals were ready to go. Of course they were. How many times would any self-respecting group of individuals allow themselves to be called the kind of names that Phillips hurled at them? Of course Molina snapped. He had been provoked. I don't think a tough-guy catcher likes being called a "bitch" by Phillips.

What Phillips didn't know is that he'd turned the screwdriver, yes, he did — but against his own team.

Phillips gave the Cardinals a shared sense of purpose. In pulling into a tie for first, the visitors rose up and smacked the Reds around for the second consecutive night. The Cardinals have won the first two games of the series by a combined 15-7 score.

Is that a statement?

"I know our guys," La Russa said. "This is not the first time we've been challenged. You just go up and down our roster and we've got a bunch of guys who are very tough characters. There are times that you beat us where we're not good enough. But you're never going to scare us. And we're never going to back down."

Conversely, the Reds became unglued Tuesday, making three errors and poor decisions. Cueto — who was kicking at Cardinals' players during the brouhaha — was completely out of steam after $5\frac{1}{3}$ innings. This would-be Bruce Lee ran out of kicks too early, after the Cardinals had pelted him for seven hits and four earned runs.

On one level, this was serious stuff. I don't think Cardinals fans enjoyed the sight of Carpenter getting bulldozed into the backstop, vulnerable to injury. Other than No. 2 catcher LaRue — who may have suffered a concussion after being kicked by the gutless Cueto — no one got hurt.

"I was in the (backstop) net with somebody kicking me from behind," Carpenter said, "... I was held down. I couldn't do anything. I wasn't throwing any punches. And we've got some guy kicking me and kicking my backup catcher in the face. He could have done some real damage. He got (LaRue) on the side of the eye, got him in his nose, got him in his face. Totally unprofessional. Unbelievable. I've never seen anything like that. I don't know where he learned to fight."

And though Carpenter was burning, I'm still laughing at this part: an adult athlete kicking during a fight, instead of squaring up like a man? Is that the best Cueto can do? Wow.

Brandon Phillips may have a word for that. ∎

2011 – 2019

The Cardinals' Yadier Molina is mobbed by teammates after hitting a sacrifice fly in the 10th inning to score Kolten Wong and beat the Braves 5-4, Monday, Oct. 8, 2019.

CARDINALS CAN'T AFFORD TO LOSE MOLINA

By Jeff Gordon
February 22, 2012

The Cardinals simply *must* lock in Yadier Molina with a contract extension.

He knows it, his agent Melvin Roman knows it and Cardinals general manager John Mozeliak knows it. If this leverage results in Molina collecting excessive pay for his twilight years, so be it.

That is just the cost of doing business. It doesn't diminish the need to keep this cornerstone player right where he is.

Consider the factors in play:

- With Albert Pujols off to finish his career in Southern California, fans will expect the Cardinals to buck up and keep their other key players. Had Albert stayed, budgeting would have been tight. Keeping the nucleus intact would have been difficult. But Albert is gone, so there are no excuses not to keep Molina, Adam Wainwright and other vital Cards as their contracts wind down.

- Moving forward, this team will win (or lose) with its pitching. The organization has assembled an army of promising young pitchers. To fully exploit that apparent strength, the Cards will need to have a savvy, take-charge catcher behind the plate. Does anybody work the game better than Molina?

- This team doesn't have a successor in line to replace Molina. Tony Cruz appears capable of backing up, but he is a long way from being a candidate to start. The same goes for Bryan Anderson, a good hitter who is still learning to work the game. Maybe in a year the Cards will feel better about their long-term catching, but right now it appears iffy.

- There aren't a lot of impact catchers in this sport. When teams get one, they typically hang on to him. Replacing Molina through free agency or a trade would be difficult. This team may be able to replace much of Albert's offense through collective effort, but how could the Cards replace all the things Molina does for the team?

- The Molina money shouldn't get too crazy. History works against catchers getting paid. Few have ever earned more than $10 million per year. Joe Mauer's eight-year, $184 million contract is an anomaly in the industry, since Mauer is getting paid to hit. If the Cards can afford to give No. 4 starting pitcher Kyle Lohse upwards of $12 million per year, the team can certainly afford to make Molina one of the highest-paid catchers of all time.

- Mozeliak paid significant money for the twilight years of Rafael Furcal and Carlos Beltran. Some independent analysts figure he overpaid both while trying to keep the 2012 team in the hunt. So why would he suddenly turn frugal when dealing with the Molina camp? Yadier is glad to have Furcal and Beltran on his side, but he understandably wants to get paid as well.

- This team seems to have can't-miss prospects at every other position, so Mozeliak will have ample opportunity to control year-to-year payroll costs. If Shelby Miller, Carlos Martinez, Zack Cox, Kolten

Cardinals pitcher Kyle Lohse (right) talks with catcher Yadier Molina after throwing a bullpen session during Cardinals spring training Monday, Feb. 20, 2012, in Jupiter, Fla.

Wong and Oscar Taveras can all perform well as young (and thus low-paid) pros, a big catching salary will be manageable.

- Although Molina would likely fade toward the end of a four- or five-year extension, he could still offer strong leadership. His history with the various emerging pitchers would have some value, just as Chris Carpenter will have value for as long as he pitches.
- With new manager Mike Matheny settling in at the helm, the Cards don't need a nagging issue hanging over the team. Securing Molina would eliminate a potentially annoying storyline while giving a critical player some peace of mind.

All these factors point toward the Cards taking care of Molina, even if the cost makes Bill DeWitt Jr. a bit uncomfortable.

The Cards have a good thing going, even with Pujols and Tony La Russa off to other adventures. The Cards appear positioned to contend for years to come.

So why would the organization jeopardize that by haggling with such a key player?

Unless the Molina camp has absolutely ridiculous salary expectations, the Cards must resolve this matter before breaking camp. ∎

CURVE IN THE ROAD

Now teammates, Wainwright and Beltran relive the pitch that sent the Cards to the 2006 World Series

By Derrick Goold
April 1, 2012

JUPITER, Fla. — There are times when Adam Wainwright happens upon a replay of the curveball that changed his life and is transported back to that October night 5½ years ago, his senses alive with Shea Stadium. He can recall the steady rain, the hand signal catcher Yadier Molina gave him before improvising a new plan, and how the pitch that won a pennant felt leaving his fingertips.

Cardinals catcher Yadier Molina jumps for joy after Mets batter
Carlos Beltran struck out to end Game 7 of the NLCS in 2006.

There is one new sensation Wainwright gets when he watches that indelible instant he struck out New York Mets outfielder Carlos Beltran.

He's more anxious watching it than he ever was living it.

"I'm shivering with nervousness when I see it," Wainwright explains. "Gosh, this is a huge moment. You don't really understand the magnitude of the moment when you're in it. And I know how it's going to end."

Or, so he thought.

That famous breaking ball has another surprise twist in it.

The two players connected by that curve — one launched by it, the other saddled with it — went in different directions from that moment only to arrive at the same place: teammates and leading players for the 2012 Cardinals. Wainwright is the Cardinals' co-ace, a former Cy Young Award contender set to return from missing a season lost to elbow surgery. Beltran is the Cardinals' big-ticket offseason acquisition, a six-time All-Star on a quest for a championship. Together they are two pillars of the team's plan to weather the absence of Albert Pujols and remain competitive. Together they already share a revered place in Cardinals history. That curve is a bend in both of their careers.

On Oct. 19, 2006, the Mets hosted the Cardinals for Game 7 of the National League Championship Series. The Cardinals led 3-1 in the bottom of the ninth when the Mets loaded the bases. With a pennant there for the taking, the Mets sent up the hitter they signed to win them one against the rookie unexpectedly thrust into the closer's role. In the span of three pitches, culminating with the curve, Wainwright became a hero, Beltran a scapegoat.

"If that's what fans want to remember about me, that's what they want to remember," Beltran says. "I bet he's thrown a lot of curveballs like that. It was just the moment. That's all. I don't live in the past. ... Move on, brother. Move on."

"It's definitely the defining moment of my career to this point," Wainwright says. "Part of that is my fault

because I loaded the bases and made it more dramatic. ... I can tell you if that at-bat goes differently I feel pretty confident saying that I wouldn't be in the same spot as I am now, I don't think. I think the fan base really embraced me after that moment. Hopefully they would have anyway, but that was a defining moment for me and such a defining moment for Cardinals baseball."

The Cardinals have won two World Series titles since that night at Shea. Wainwright has twice finished in the top three for the Cy Young Award. The curve was a turning point for the Mets, too. The Mets and Beltran have not been back to the postseason since he took the called strike 3. Injuries, ill-conceived contracts, and one investing debacle have eroded the franchise.

Whether it's fair or not, the whole hot mess is traced back to one night in 2006 when fortunes turned on a curve.

"The poor man has become the symbol of failed expectations," venerable columnist George Vecsey wrote about Beltran in The New York Times last year. "(He) personified the time with one signature called third strike to end the seventh and last game of the 2006 (NLCS). Even if he had taken one lusty 'Casey at the Bat' swing, and missed, perhaps his fate would be different. But he gawked."

Last spring, when The New Yorker writer Jeffrey Toobin asked Fred Wilpon if the Mets are cursed, the principal owner answered by mimicking Beltran's flinch at Wainwright's curveball.

This is what life looks like on opposite ends of that curveball.

Wainwright is celebrated, with longtime friend Skip Schumaker saying that pitch "sent him off" to the elite status he now has. Beltran is the target of an inside joke from the owner and, as former teammate David Wright explained this spring, unjustly "vilified."

"It would have meant more for us if I would have gotten the hit, I guess," Beltran says. "In this game, you're going to experience good things, you're going to experience bad things. The players who are capable of being consistent are the players who don't let the negative affect them. You have to move on. ... No one likes to walk a hitter with the bases loaded. Nobody likes to go up there and strike out with the guys in scoring in position.

"But it's not a matter of if," Beltran concludes. "It's going to happen. It is going to happen. You are going to have a moment when you fail."

BELTRAN'S BEST

Beltran was in that spot against Wainwright because of his success, especially against the Cardinals. The switch-hitting center fielder burned through records in the 2004 postseason with Houston and torched the Cardinals with a .417 average, a .958 slugging percentage, four homers and 12 runs scored in a seven-game NLCS the Astros lost. That winter, Beltran signed a seven-year, $119 million deal with the Mets that established him as the bat that would bring them October glory.

The 2006 season was the return on that investment.

"That year," Beltran said, "was my best year in baseball."

Beltran hit a career-high 41 homers that season, drove in a career-high 116 runs, had a career-high .594 slugging percentage and finished a career-best fourth in the NL MVP voting. He propelled a 2006 Mets club that scored the third-most runs (834) and had the third-best ERA (4.14) in the league. They finished 97-65, nine games ahead of any other team in the NL. These Mets entered October as the favorite to win the title and swept the division series to set up one of the most lopsided NLCS ever in terms of record, vs. the 83-win Cardinals.

At the time, the Mets felt this was the first of many trips to October for this lineup, and that Beltran was a reason.

"He was everything that we wanted him to be," Wright recalls.

The Mets were poised to replace the Cardinals as the perennial playoff team. After back-to-back 100-win seasons in 2004 and 2005, the Cardinals inched into the playoffs on the final day of the regular season despite losing nine of their final 12 games.

The Cardinals were vulnerable, and the apparent heirs were eager to ascend. The Mets defeated Chris Carpenter in Game 6 to get a shot at becoming the 12th consecutive home team to force a decisive Game 7 and win it. Endy Chavez robbed a homer from Scott Rolen in the top of the sixth. But Jeff Suppan pitched out of a bases-loaded boondoggle in the bottom, and Yadier Molina gave the Cardinals a 3-1 lead with a home run in the top of the ninth.

That brought Wainwright. The Mets got two quick singles, and with two outs Wainwright walked Paul Lo Duca to load the bases.

Beltran stepped in.

Wainwright took a breath.

"He made three of the best pitches he probably made that year," Wright says. "It almost felt like we had a lot of momentum and he really bore down and said it was going to end right there."

THREE PITCHES, 67 SECONDS

Wainwright's head was swimming in the din. It felt like he could hear every fan yelling at him. The first two batters had reached on singles. Pitching coach Dave Duncan had just visited the mound, and Josh Kinney and Tyler Johnson were warming in the bullpen. He admitted later that he was "overwhelmed by the situation."

By the time Beltran came to the plate, Wainwright had thrown 25 pitches, six of which were curveballs. Both of the outs he had came on curveballs — a 75 mph bender that froze Cliff Floyd and a 74 mph hook Jose Reyes lined into center. With Beltran coming up, Molina trotted out to plot their approach.

"We're going to go sinker down and away and get ahead on the first pitch," Molina whispered to Wainwright, his mouth covered by his glove. "We'll go from there."

Wainwright replied: "Perfect."

Molina trotted back toward home plate.

That's when the catcher changed his mind.

First pitch - 83 mph changeup, down the middle.

When he got in his squat behind the plate, Molina waved to Wainwright and tapped his chest protector with both hands. Wainwright read it as the universal sign for, "Trust me." He no longer wanted a fastball. He called for a changeup.

"Feelings," Molina explained years later.

"Hitters are a lot more aggressive, so you can make the sinker down and away, but there's a rookie on the mound and you're looking for something to get them off balance that looks like a heater," Wainwright says. "I think it just caught him off. ... In that situation, that's my fourth-best pitch. There's no way he could be looking for that."

Beltran says he wasn't: "Normally, first pitch you're going to get a fastball away, and he threw me a changeup."

That Beltran took a pitch or fell behind in the count was not unusual. In his previous 30 plate appearances in the series, Beltran had fallen behind on the first pitch 21 times. In total, Beltran would swing and miss on only six pitches during the entire series. He would take 34 strikes, including a first-pitch strike 15 times. He would also work his way back into the count each time and go five for 18 with two strikes on him. Two of his three homers came on two-strike pitches, two of them came after he fell behind 0-1.

"That's the genius behind it," Wainwright says. "I think the whole at-bat changed with the changeup first pitch strike Yadier called. I also think if I had given up a double right there to clear the bases, Tony La Russa would have strangled me and I would have died."

Second pitch - 76 mph curveball, down and in.

Going into the at-bat, Wainwright and Molina made the same promise, individually. If they got ahead with the first pitch, Beltran was going to have to beat the Cardinals on Wainwright's curveball. It was, is and because of this moment probably always will be his best pitch. He'd snapped it by Floyd earlier and had only thrown one in the inning that hovered. The curve is Wainwright's great equalizer and, as Schumaker says, "The whole league knows that."

Beltran had just yet to see it.

"I wasn't thinking about Carlos," Molina says. "I was thinking about Waino. Waino's curveball is not easy to hit, so if we're going to lose that game it had to be on the curveball, no matter what."

Though Wainwright had finished two previous games in the series, this was Beltran's first look at the rookie closer. The second pitch was his first look at the curve. Wainwright fired it to the inside third of the plate on the lefthanded-hitting Beltran, and the Mets' center fielder fouled it off his front foot.

The tying run was at second, the winning run at first, and he was down 0-2.

"Sometimes you think it's a pitch to hit," Beltran says, "and you're not going to be able to square every single ball."

Final pitch - 74 mph curveball, outside edge.

Wainwright had studied Beltran throughout the series in preparation for a duel like this. He had seen Beltran fall behind 0-2 or 1-2 in 15 previous plate appearances. Ten times the next pitch was a ball. He had no intention of letting the All-Star back in the at-bat that way. So as Molina patted the dirt behind the plate with his glove, Wainwright released the most important pitch of his career.

"There was," he says, "a lot of conviction behind it."

Wainwright's curve usually travels in that 73- to 75-mph range, and it has been measured with an average drop of 55 inches. This pitch started above Beltran's shoulders and plummeted into the strike zone, tickling the outside edge of the plate and aimed to land just off the back corner of the plate. Lance Berkman, who was watching on TV, said, "That pitch started out 5 feet over his head." Wright and others called it unhittable. Home plate Tim Welke called it a strike as Molina gloved it.

"It was like, 'Did my TV skip? Did I miss a pitch?'" says John Smoltz, a mentor for Wainwright. "It was the perfect pitch at the perfect time to the perfect place and there was nothing the hitter could have done with it. He could have told Carlos the curve was coming and it would still be a bowel-breaker."

Beltran's bat didn't come off his shoulder.

Game over. Fates cast.

The whole at-bat took 67 seconds of a 3-hour, 23-minute game.

"I wasn't thinking about Carlos, I was thinking about Waino. Waino's curveball is not easy to hit, so if we're going to lose that game it had to be on the curveball, no matter what."

—Yadier Molina

"I couldn't pull the trigger," Beltran says. "It happened many times before in my career. It just happened in a playoff situation. I don't think it was unhittable. I wasn't prepared for it. ... I couldn't react to it. He got me."

The next day, among the messages of support Beltran received from friends came one from Cali Magallanes, Mets' baseball chapel minister. Beltran confirmed he replied to it with seven words: "It's OK, brother. God is in control." The outfielder does not like to talk about the at-bat. He'll field questions about it politely but redirect them toward the future.

He admitted to watching a replay of the at-bat only once — the next day. He wanted to see if there was something he could have done differently.

"I wouldn't change anything," he says. "It was a good pitch."

TEAMMATES NOW

The two had never spoken and had only had awkward silences passing each other at ballparks since that game. When Beltran agreed to a two-year, $26 million deal to be the Cardinals' starting right fielder, Wainwright figured it was time. He got Beltran's number from a team official and left a message. A few hours later, Beltran called back. A few minutes into the conversation, Wainwright brought up the curve.

"I said, 'Brother, don't even worry about that,'" Beltran recalls. "I don't even talk about it anymore."

"I wanted to make sure that we would be comfortable standing in the same room together, that

there wasn't anything underlying there," Wainwright says. "When you're teammates with somebody ... you need impact players on the same page."

Wainwright was so aware of the curve between them that when he faced Beltran this spring in drills he did not throw him a breaking ball. His fear was a fan would yell, "Hey, remember that, Carlos?" Wainwright has always tried to remember Beltran when discussing that game. Had his pitch broken differently or frozen another player, their careers would not be linked, their destinies mixed.

But they are, two sides of the same curve.

Wainwright knows that the "defining" pitch of his career wouldn't be without Beltran. It was a great pitch at a great time on a great stage that had a great result against a great player. Subtract Beltran from that moment and it loses some of its greatness. Taking that curveball does not make Beltran a lesser player. The curveball is memorable because of how good Beltran is.

"I don't think there's anything wrong with recounting that moment because for me that's my favorite that I've ever been involved in in baseball," Wainwright says. "But there's a certain level of respect that has to come with that. It's not nearly as climactic, it's not nearly as dramatic without him because of his history against the Cardinals and how great he is. That helps make it."

Wainwright doesn't know how this will end.

He just knows it won't be against Beltran.

It could be with him. ■

ONE STOPPER, 3 BOPPERS

Wainwright keeps Phils from sweep; Molina, Beltran, Adams hit homers

By Derrick Goold
May 28, 2012

On a Cardinals club that is trying to regain its health and fumbling for a grip during a tumble where the results have been as ragged as the execution, starter Adam Wainwright knows how that funk feels.

He's been there, done that, and had the ERA to prove it.

He also found a way out.

Offering his teammates comfort as he rolls with revived confidence, Wainwright muscled the Cardinals to an 8-3 victory Sunday against the Philadelphia Phillies at Busch Stadium. Three home runs backed the righthander as he kept the Phillies from what would have been their first four-game sweep of the Cardinals in St. Louis in 99 years.

"I definitely had the mind-set that the Phillies were not going to sweep us," said Wainwright, who limited Philadelphia to a run on seven hits in six innings. "By looking what our team did, our team had the same outlook and the same pregame thought as I did. They weren't going to come into our place and sweep four games from us. That's for sure."

The win was the Cardinals first at home this season against a National League East foe in seven tries, and it sends them off on a 10-game road trip that starts with seven against winning teams. Sunday's victory was the Cardinals' first against an opponent with a winning record coming into that game since they defeated the 2-1 Cincinnati Reds on April 9. The Cardinals were 0-7 since against teams with winning records on the day they played.

For the first time since he lost to the Cardinals and Chris Carpenter in Game 5 of last fall's National League division series, Phillies ace Roy Halladay had his rematch. But Sunday's "heavyweight bout" Cardinals manager Mike Matheny expected between Halladay and Wainwright didn't develop because Halladay was knocked out after two innings. Yadier Molina's grand slam in the first inning did it on the scoreboard. Shoulder tightness in the second did it on the field.

Molina's third grand slam of his career was the fifth Halladay (4-5) had allowed in his career in 155 chances opponents have had with the bases loaded.

"We needed that spark," Matheny said. "It seems like we've been fighting out of a hole consistently here for a while."

In eight of the previous nine games, the Cardinals had fallen behind first. Six times, including two times this series against the Phillies, they rallied to tie or take the lead.

But they only won two of those six games.

"They're not oblivious to the fact that we've fought from behind a lot — which I love, absolutely love — but then the end part of that you can't help but realize is we're still on the losing end," the manager said. "If you're not careful you can lose some of that fight."

All eight of the Cardinals' runs Sunday came on home runs. Molina drove an 0-1 fastball from Halladay to one of the deepest points of the park to start the show of force. Carlos Beltran followed with a three-run blast that gave him the league lead in homers with 15 and a share of the RBI lead with 41. Rookie Matt Adams punctuated the win in the sixth with his first big-league homer, a solo bolt.

That gave Wainwright (4-5) ample cushion he didn't need.

The only times in the past 10 games that the Cardinals have scored first have been Wainwright's two starts. With a shutout of San Diego and the lockdown of the Phillies, Wainwright has slashed his ERA from 5.77 to 4.45 in 15 innings. He's done so with the feel for a new fastball and the help of Rafael Furcal.

The Cardinals' shortstop made three slick defensive plays Sunday — a diving catch of a slicing line drive, an on-his-back flip for a force out at second, and a daring throw home. With Carlos Ruiz at third in the second inning, Furcal fielded a sharp grounder to his right and fired home instead of to first. His throw caught Ruiz and kept the Phillies scoreless.

"It's a crazy play," Furcal said, "but I love to do it."

In his shutout, Wainwright reintroduced the four-seam fastball to his repertoire. He had not thrown it consistently since Class AA but found faith in it against the Padres. With it, Wainwright was able to get both velocity and movement on the pitch. Molina said

Yadier Molina rounds the bases after hitting a first-inning grand slam off Roy Halladay.

Wainwright became "more confident, more aggressive" because of the pitch.

His cutter, which has been misbehaving all season — and clocking in at 84 mph — had more life Sunday, and he hit 88 mph with it.

"Now that I'm rolling again, my grip does all the work. I set it and forget it like that (rotisserie) machine," Wainwright said. "And my approach to the (four-seam) is just to fire it and let it work. That mentality has really helped my (cutter). I'm throwing it with the same intensity. ... I like where I am right now.

"The old me is the new me."

That's all the Cardinals seek as a team. ∎

BEST CATCHERS IN THEIR FIELD

Cards' Molina and Giants' Posey have become difference-makers who each have keyed their team's success

By Derrick Goold
October 17, 2012

A bat in hand, San Francisco Giants cleanup hitter Buster Posey had only a minute to spare Monday before his turn came to work on a swing that will win awards and make him millions. He used it to consider the Cardinals Yadier Molina, a fellow catcher, and what he does so well with the less glamorous tools of their trade.

"Everything," Posey said.

He shifted to lean on his bat on a dugout step.

"I know that sounds cliché. I do," he continued. "But he receives well. He blocks well. He throws well, and he commands a pitching staff really well. All the things he does and some intangibles that he does in there as well that you can't really put numbers on. He does everything. ... The goal is to give those pitchers as much as confidence as you can. You know everybody on the field is looking to you for it."

Everybody in and around this series is, too.

The National League championship series that pits two of the league's oldest franchises and its past two pennant winners also highlights the two best catchers in their field.

This has become an October that celebrates the crouch. All four of baseball's remaining playoff teams are managed by a former catcher, and all four teams feature an All-Star behind the plate.

In the NLCS, which shifts to Busch Stadium for Game 3 of the best-of-seven series this afternoon (weather permitting), the Giants' Posey is poised to win his first Silver Slugger award as the best offensive player at the position while Molina is bound to win the Gold Glove Award, his fifth consecutive as the best defensive player at their position.

Both have been the most reliable producer for their playoff teams, lifting their masks and rising from their squats into consideration for the most valuable player.

"I think you're talking about two of the best catchers in the game when you're looking at Yadi and Buster, two guys who catch well, throw well, handle the bat, hit for power," said Giants manager and former catcher Bruce Bochy. "They have the whole game. And so it's a big reason why these two teams are here."

With his .336 batting average, Posey, the favorite to win the MVP, is the first backstop in the league to win the batting title since 1942. A former first-round draft pick, Posey surged when other catchers tire, batting .385 with a .646 slugging percentage and collecting 60 of his 103 RBIs after the All-Star break. He returns from a violent collision at the plate that ended his 2011 season with a broken fibula and wrecked ankle to probably become the first NL catcher to win the MVP award since Johnny Bench did so in 1972.

Molina is set to receive enough votes to be the first Cardinals catcher since Tim McCarver in 1967 to finish in the MVP's top five. Molina set highs for home runs (22), average (.315), RBIs (76), and almost every other offensive category. Molina didn't have a single month this season where his on-base percentage or slugging percentage was lower than his career average. He coupled that breakout with the usual defensive prowess, which includes a couple teams in the NL admitting they don't run on him.

"We're all better because of Yadier Molina behind the plate," said Cardinals manager Mike Matheny, a four-time Gold Glove-winner at catcher.

Although they come at the position from different directions — Posey the gifted hitter who has improved as a receiver; Molina the preternatural catcher who has willed himself to be a better hitter — they arrive at the NLCS with commonalities.

Both made an early October mark as rookies. Posey, the 2010 NL rookie of the year, boosted the Giants to the World Series title. At 22, Molina started Game 4 of the 2004 World Series for the Cardinals and in the fourth inning jawed with eventual MVP Manny Ramirez over a dispute on ethics.

"He's had that edge since he came up and that's what makes him such a great player," Cardinals pitcher Chris Carpenter said.

Echoed Bochy on his backstop: "We saw in 2010 what a difference-maker Buster Posey can be for us. We put a lot on him at that time, at his age, his lack of experience. We went on to win the World Series because of his bat and how well he caught."

Both also have a tie to Matheny.

The former Cardinals catcher is fond of telling the story of how he saw Molina at spring training one year and returned home to tell his wife he "saw the kid who is going to take my job." Matheny went to the Giants because Molina did for 2005. Before his career ended there, Matheny heard about the kid catcher with the big bat. Matheny spoke with young Buster about maintaining strength at the most-demanding position.

"I think these are your selections for most valuable player, right here," Matheny said. "There's so many things about Yadi Molina that you really can't classify or measure by the metrics. ... You tell him that he can't do something, he's going to find a way to prove you wrong. Tell him he can't run, he's going to lead the league in stolen bases as a catcher. You tell him he can't hit for power, he's going to hit 20."

And often his team will follow.

The last thing Posey said before trotting away to hit is how a catcher has to lead a team. It's "expected," he said. Molina seconded that, calling Posey "a leader" before he said anything about his hitting.

That's what differentiates these two catchers beyond the numbers. They have a gravitational pull. Their team orbits around them.

"Who do you want up with the game on the line? Who do you want to count on at that moment?" asked Giants infielder Ryan Theriot, who has played with both. "I think you could probably look up and down each lineup and Yadier and Buster are going to be at the top of your list. That speaks a lot about those two guys and how the teams feed off them. ...

"They set the tone. It all starts with them." ■

Although they come at the position from different directions they arrive at the NLCS with commonalities.

Cardinals catcher Yadier Molina has been a force behind the plate and now is doing the same at bat, as he leads the National League in hitting.

MOLINA'S SUCCESS LONG IN MAKING

He has risen from amateur team in Puerto Rico to an MVP-caliber player

By Derrick Goold
June 9, 2013

CINCINNATI — When Yadier Molina still was a teenager, his father, Benjamin, placed him on an amateur team in Puerto Rico that pitted his youngest son against men 10 years older and 10 years more mature and forced him to find a way to make sure they weren't also 10 years better.

The team was the Hatillo Tigres.

Benjamin had another predator in mind.

"I threw him with the lions," he would say.

That was the explanation that Benjamin gave Bengie and Jose Molina, the older brothers, when they asked their dad why young Yadier was urged to play in one of Puerto Rico's top men's amateur leagues before even being eligible for the major-league draft.

"Oh, I'm going to throw him with the lions and make him grow up," Bengie Molina recalled his father saying. "And he did. Yadi did. That's why I think he's good. He had to be a veteran at a young age. When he came over here it was nothing. I think that's what started it, at least. You have to grow up quick in that league. That's the way I saw it. That was the first step to where he is now."

Where he is now is the MVP-caliber catcher and compass for the team with the best record in baseball. The Cardinals often go where Molina points them.

If it's not shepherding a rookie-infused rotation to the lowest ERA in the National League, it's providing as the leading hitter, often in the middle of the lineup.

Molina walked into the ballpark Saturday with a .352 average, the highest in the NL and second in baseball only to Triple Crown-winner Miguel Cabrera.

He took over the NL lead with four consecutive two-hit games to end a week that began with his ejection from a game and one-game suspension. Major League Baseball excused Molina's spiking of his helmet and fixated more on the contact he made with an umpire and a past suspension for an aggressive confrontation with an umpire. The Cardinals pointed to Molina's aggressive argument with a rookie umpire as a sign of his intensity, his competitiveness.

Those traits, teammates suggest, fuel his performance on the field and his increasing presence off it. They cannot be spliced. The high batting average and MVP trappings are recent additions to his game, but they are rooted in the same qualities that have made Molina the heir to Albert Pujols as the Cardinals' best player.

His brother said that mature burn and feel for leading started with the Tigres. Chris Carpenter said the world first saw it when young Molina confronted Manny Ramirez at home plate in the 2004 World Series. Adam Wainwright believes it was a more recent event that crystallized Molina's place in the clubhouse — for him and the team.

It happened where he spent the weekend at Great American Ball Park.

"In my mind, it's the Cincinnati ordeal," Wainwright said of an August 2010 brawl that has become the B-roll for the rivalry with the Reds.

"Brandon Phillips had taunted our team a little bit, and we know Phillips — he feeds off that negative whatever. He tapped Yadier's shinguards, and Yadi didn't take that. So he kicked his bat. That said, 'You disrespect me, you disrespect our team?' For me that was a big moment for him. That was kind of what put it over the top for me.

"Yadier has come into his own."

Molina does not see his rise to prominence at the plate or on the team in these snapshots, tiny epiphanies captured by the camera. It was far more glacial.

Molina joined the Cardinals as a fourth-round pick out of high school in Puerto Rico in 2000.

He reached the majors in 2004, spending time as a backup to his mentor, current manager Mike Matheny. By 2005, Matheny was in San Francisco and Molina was the starter. He won his first of two World Series with the team in 2006 and his public accomplishments are tattooed on his arms, from Gold Gloves to titles. Comfort off the field came slower than it did on the field.

"When I came up I was here in the corner, watching and trying to learn and listening to what (veteran players) had to say, seeing how they managed, how they led," Molina said. "At the time I was just watching and listening and keeping all of that information in my mind. I didn't know the language well. It was hard for me to communicate with another person, to have that conversation one-on-one. But over time I've learned. I've learned the language.

"And when I was more comfortable, I had that information to put to work."

His swing like his presence took time. Molina was the man of many stances, mimicking one of his brothers one day and Pujols the next. As he improved his nutrition and his fitness during the offseason, he also settled into one approach at the plate. The results have been a .301 batting average and a .780 on-base-plus-slugging-percentage in his previous 730 games. No everyday catcher in the majors has a higher average and more than 300 games at catcher since 2008. And he's improving.

Yadier Molina rounds first base after launching a solo home run against the Brewers.

Every month last season his on-base percentage and slugging was higher than his career average. He hit .394 in May. Reigning MVP Buster Posey was the next closest NL catcher, at .305.

"I feel I am getting better every year," Molina said. "I know myself."

Finding the words to describe what Molina knows and how he has gone from the finest defensive catcher in the game to one of the finest all-around players is when teammates rely on stories not statistics. Matheny said Molina does "something every day to help us win that stats do not give due credit."

There was the time Molina and Tony Cruz came in early to put together new scouting reports on Washington hitters. Or how Molina will sometimes stop referring to starting pitchers by their names and just say, "We."

Bengie talked about the lessons from being thrown to the Tigres. Wainwright talked about confronting Phillips. Carpenter said it's fruitless to try to come up with the one example or one anecdote or one moment to define what Molina has become to the Cardinals.

They all fall short.

"As many questions as you want to ask to try and describe who and how he is and what he brings to this team, there is always going to be something left out," Carpenter said. "That's how good he is. There is always something that is missed. There is no way to get everything into an answer that describes the total package of Yadi. We can go from on the field to off the field and into the clubhouse, on to the bus, on the plane, anywhere, and even at a team function or a golf tournament when he doesn't even play golf. We can talk about each of those things and there will always be something we miss.

"That's because he is the total package of what it means to be a great player." ∎

BENCHMARK ACHIEVEMENT

Cardinals' Molina gets ringing endorsement from Hall of Fame catcher

By Derrick Goold
July 7, 2013

Wherever he was in Italy on an early-summer getaway last month, Hall of Fame catcher Johnny Bench still found Wi-Fi access that kept him connected to the games back home. He stayed "on top" of his Cincinnati Reds and saw the rise of a few rookie sensations. He joked that only the Texas Rangers' sweep of the Cardinals and the Pittsburgh Pirates' surge escaped his notice.

Who didn't fail to get his attention was someone he's watched for a while.

Yadier Molina has his attention.

"He's a force," Bench told the Post-Dispatch from his home in Naples, Fla. "He's the most dangerous guy on that team. He's become one of the most dangerous guys in the league. He is the complete package."

Through Saturday's games, the Cardinals' catcher led the National League in hitting (.346) and doubles (26), and that evening he became the second consecutive catcher to lead the National League in All-Star votes. Molina received 6,883,258 votes to edge teammate Carlos Beltran for the overall lead and secure his fifth consecutive All-Star selection. His status for the game will be clearer Sunday after scans taken of his irritated right knee will determine the cause and extent of the soreness that kept him out of Saturday's victory.

He is the fifth Cardinal to be elected to three All-Star Game starting lineups and only the fifth NL catcher with at least three starts since fans began determining the starters. In the eight decades of the All-Star Game, only 10 NL catchers have appeared in more than five All-Star games.

At the top is Bench with 12.

Bench, the greatest catcher of them all, blended prowess at the plate with virtuosity behind it. He won two MVPs, earned 13 consecutive All-Star selections (though he did not appear in all the games) and merited 10 Gold Glove awards, second only to Ivan Rodriguez's 13. Bench is the standard. Bench, 65, also is a catching connoisseur and what he watches to see he often does in the Cardinals' 30-year-old backstop.

"I judge a guy by how he calls his game and the respect he gets from the pitchers after the game," Bench said. "You can see it in the hugs. There's a real concert going on there. They trust him. They key off of him. As a catcher, you're the artist and they're the brush. All you're doing is painting a picture. … You put that with the hitting and it's clear he finally got comfortable with what he wanted to do. He has redefined himself. All of a sudden there's been this little more respect for him as a result.

"It's like they just figured out he's really damn good."

MVP CANDIDACY

Molina is being positioned as an MVP-caliber catcher this season, a candidacy that gained momentum last season when Giants catcher Buster Posey won the trophy. Molina had career highs in batting average (.315), home runs (22), RBIs (76) and slugging percentage (.501).

Baseball's new calculus loved him.

According to FanGraphs, Molina's 139 weighted runs created — a measure of a player's offensive value in terms of runs — was better than all but four of Bench's best offensive years. Molina's 6.9 Wins Above Replacement in 2012 were the 10th highest single-season total for an NL catcher in baseball's expansion era. Bench has three of the top six, and Posey's 7.4 WAR last season ranks sixth in that span.

It's heady company that "he always had," Bench said. "But all of a sudden you have a catcher hitting third or fourth or fifth like Buster and (Molina), and that brings credibility."

While building a defensive and durable reputation, Bench also led the league in RBIs three times and retired with 389 home runs.

He holds the single-season records among catchers for homers and RBIs and ranks second and third, respectively, for career totals in those power numbers. He can relate to the difficulty of maintaining offensive production while playing as a catcher. He had six broken bones in his foot. Missed two days.

He broke fingers. Kept hitting. The type of sturdiness that Molina has achieved by trimming weight and improving nutrition, Bench said he came by naturally from his days hoisting peanuts sacks and cotton sacks as a boy.

"Great back muscles," he said.

Great coordination, too. During the course of a 30-minute conversation, Bench tied a catcher's ability to read and react behind the plate and deliver a strong throw to the fast-twitch needed to see and identify a pitch to deliver a solid swing. He was able to do both, well.

Other catchers struggle to connect the two. He also believes the two disciplines benefited from the one approach he always tried to have.

"This was my inner-conceit: I was better than the situation," Bench said. "The pitcher couldn't get me out. The runner couldn't steal on me. You have to feel that way to be better."

COOPERSTOWN CORNER

The offensive side of the game has come later to Molina than contemporaries such as Posey and Joe Mauer and recent standouts at the position like Ivan Rodriguez and Mike Piazza.

Posey won the NL batting title last season, the first full-time catcher do so since 1942.

Mauer has three of them in the American League. With the league lead now, Molina would echo Posey and this season would continue Molina's midcareer incline of production. Through the prism of increased performance at the plate, Bench said Molina's whole game appears sharper, better, even though he's always been superb.

During the conversation, it's Bench who brings up Cooperstown.

There are 13 catchers who played in the major leagues who have been inducted into the National Baseball Hall of Fame, and Rodriguez will go before the voters soon. Bench does the math and suggests that's one for every decade, about one for every generation.

"They don't come along often," he said.

SIMMONS COMPARISON

Bench sat on the 16-member committee that considered Cardinals great Ted Simmons' candidacy for the Hall in December 2010. Simmons did not get in despite his only crime apparently being he was second-best to Bench. Bench lobbied for his teammate Dave Concepcion in that meeting, arguing that he was second-best to Ozzie Smith.

Different position, different players, similar plights. Only Simmons has more RBIs as a Cardinals catcher than Molina and more home runs, but he has way more. In RBIs Simmons leads Molina 929-511, and in homers it's 172-83.

Bench starts doing the math. Can Molina get to 1,000 RBIs? What about 2,000 hits? Will Molina stay durable enough to be behind the plate enough and still solid at it.

Bench will be watching.

"His defense speaks for itself and it always has, but now his offense is bringing him attention," Bench said. "He's driving in big runs. He's a very tough out. He kills this team. He kills that team. Balls are going all over. … Now people really start looking what's possible. Now is when the microscope comes out. He'll get the attention and those honors will follow. The numbers will total up. The home runs will total up and then we'll see.

"If he stays healthy," the Hall of Famer concludes, "call me in 10 years."

Bench offered one piece of advice for Molina. It wasn't so much a suggestion as a request.

The Hall of Famer chuckled as he said it.

"Don't beat the Reds." ∎

Yadier Molina guns a throw to second moments before a recent game. Molina is among the All-Stars this week in New York, where his clutch performance led the Cardinals past the Mets in Game 7 of the 2006 NLCS.

BIG NIGHT IN BIG APPLE

Molina's star first shone with playoff performance against Mets

By Derrick Goold
July 16, 2013

NEW YORK — The moments from Game 7 of the 2006 National League championship series between the Cardinals and the New York Mets are captured in photos, posters, and even an etching on a brick outside the ballpark that replaced Shea Stadium. Endy Chavez's dazzling leap to rob a home run. Jeff Suppan holding the NLCS MVP trophy. Scott Rolen weeping. Carlos Beltran taking. Adam Wainwright triumphant.

The snapshots are so clear that it's easy to miss the bigger picture.

That game, a teammate said years later, "was all about Yadi."

That was the night baseball met Yadier Molina.

"The moment, the whole game, those will always be in my heart," Molina said this past weekend. "If I need it, it's always in my heart."

The 84th All-Star Game brings Molina back to Queens as the star of stars, back to the borough of his breakthrough. Entering that rain-soaked series, Molina was the Cardinals' defense-first catcher, a heralded glove with an uncertain bat who privately made that October a personal quest to prove otherwise. He would not allow his .216 average in the regular season to define him. Instead, Game 7 did.

Molina guided MVP Suppan through a treacherous inning. Molina called the sequence of pitches for Wainwright that ended with the curveball that froze Beltran. And Molina drilled the two-run homer in the ninth inning that was the difference between going home and going on to the World Series.

The player who left Shea Stadium that night returns tonight to Citi Field, the new Mets' ballpark, as perhaps the game's most complete player and one of its most popular.

Molina leads the National League with a .341 average, has widely been picked as the first half MVP by pundits, and received the most fan All-Star votes of any player in the NL. His jersey is the third-highest seller in baseball behind retiring closer Mariano Rivera and reigning NL MVP Buster Posey. His peers and opponents have run out of adjectives.

"He does everything," Posey said.

"He is as good as it gets on the defensive side," former MVP and Twins catcher Joe Mauer said. "And now he's swinging the bat well. He's one of the best around."

"He has to be the best in the game, right?" Wainwright said.

"He's such a dynamic catcher a lot of time people overlook that he's a great hitter, a clutch hitter," Washington manager Davey Johnson said Monday as the All-Star festivities began with the Home Run Derby. "To me, it's his durability and his catching that really set him apart. I love the way he handles the staff. I love Posey. I love (Brian) McCann. But this guy's the horse."

Molina, who turned 31 this past week, had a career year last season with a .315 average, a .501 slugging percentage, 22 homers and 76 RBIs. Not once in a single month in 2012 was his slugging percentage lower than his career average. He's improved upon that this season. With four hits Sunday night at Wrigley Field, Molina raised his average to .341. With teammate Allen Craig's .333 nipping at his heels, Molina is trying to become the first Cardinal since Albert Pujols to lead the team in hitting for three consecutive seasons.

Molina's three-run homer Sunday night capped a 10-6 victory during which he had a home run, three runs, four hits and four RBIs.

Since the start of the 2012 season, Molina's .325 average ranks fourth in baseball behind Miguel Cabrera, Posey and Joey Votto. They have each won an MVP in the previous three seasons. And even baseball's higher math adores Molina. Molina's Wins Above Replacement (WAR) — a statistic that aims to measure how much a player's total game adds to his teams win total — was 6.9 in 2012. That's the 11th-highest ever for a catcher.

That doesn't begin to measure his value like one late-night flight can.

When he joined several teammates on a private jet to Anaheim for the 2010 All-Star Game, it was Molina who stayed quietly on the side and listened to Pujols talk about dressing the part of an All-Star and other suggestions. On the flight from Chicago late Sunday night, it was five-time All-Star Molina and Carlos Beltran who held court, talking baseball for two hours, sharing insights.

"It's happened fast," said Wainwright, who was on board. "He's always had those leadership qualities. It's just now is the right time to put that forward. We need him to be the Yadier that we've come to know. He's the team leader, the heart and soul of our team. He's amazing. It's something that has happened naturally as his game has evolved. He started off as a great-catching, soft-hitting guy and now his game is complete."

That's how Molina has come to define his role. Complete.

He learned it from coach Dave Ricketts, the longtime Cardinals minor-league instructor who is credited with developing generations of catchers and establishing the team's tradition behind the plate. Cardinals catchers have won 11 of the past 22 Gold Gloves at the position.

"That's one of the things he approached me about — to be a good leader, to get respect" Molina said Monday at Citi Field, still wearing his sunglasses as he met the assembled reporters. "Whenever you're out

Yadier Molina celebrates his go-ahead, two-run homer in the ninth inning of Game 7 of the 2006 NLCS with Albert Pujols.

there catching you're like the captain of the team. If you feel down that day, you cannot show that to your team. That's going to bring down the team. You have to be the leader. It's all about the game, the whole game. Not only on the field, but in the clubhouse, outside the lines, off the field, in the city. Wherever."

That about describes Game 7.

Molina kept Suppan calm when Rolen's error nearly cost the Cardinals the game. He kept Wainwright on task with the bases loaded and the All-Star Beltran at the plate. He switched to a changeup after telling the rookie he was going to call for a fastball. "Trust me," he pantomimed. And there, on national television, he had the clutch home run introduced him to October lore.

Cardinals manager Mike Matheny listened to that Game 7 on the road as he drove to a farm outside of St. Louis because "deer season was hot" and there was hunting to be done. He got to a TV in time to see Molina's home run. General manager John Mozeliak, who was at Shea, said that was "the moment in time he seized. It was poignant." Older brother Bengie

Molina was watching the game from his home, pacing. He knew the Mets pitcher Aaron Heilman was going to start with a changeup and talked to the TV, pleading with his brother to be ready.

"Don't miss it. Don't miss it," Bengie recalled. "Be ready. Don't miss it. And he hit it out. I started crying. Very emotional day."

Yadier grinned broadly this past weekend at the memory of Game 7 when asked if that game changed anything for him.

"It changed one thing," he said. "I have a ring."

A Gold Glove came two years after Game 7 and his first All-Star invitation and MVP vote three years later. And now he takes the stage as arguably the games best.

"From a long time ago I knew he was going to special in this league," Bengie Molina said. "It didn't have to be 2004. It didn't have to be there in Game 7. I think over and over and over again he's proved that's what he is. It's not one play. It's not that one night that says what he is. He's kept proving it and proving it from that day on." ∎

WORLD SERIES X4

Molina will join elite group when he starts Wednesday

By Derrick Goold
October 22, 2013

BOSTON — On the eve of Game 4 in the 2004 World Series, the game he would replace catcher Mike Matheny in the starting lineup, Yadier Molina left the ballpark understanding he would get his first World Series start because he had been paired with Jason Marquis for a while. Manager Tony La Russa offered another explanation publicly, saying Matheny would be "fresh for tomorrow" and a Game 5 — which would never happen.

Matheny, nine years later, can still see through the sugarcoating.

"It wasn't the first time in my career something like that happened to me. First time in a World Series that it did," said Matheny, who fills out the lineups these days as the Cardinals' manager. "Obviously I saw how special Yadi was going to be. I knew it would be a long career for him. … I think it was clear we needed to do something different."

On Oct. 27, 2004, the Cardinals trailed the steamrolling Boston Red Sox three games to none in the Fall Classic, and Molina took his spot in the lineup, batting eighth after John Mabry, now the team's hitting coach. Matheny, a pending free agent,

wouldn't start another game for the Cardinals. The Red Sox won the title that night, but in St. Louis that game had resonance — the ceremonial passing of the mask, one Gold Glove award-winner to the next. Molina's start that night was the beginning of what may be remembered as an era.

When Molina starts Game 1 of this year's World Series on Wednesday at Fenway Park, he'll appear in his fourth World Series, the only player of this modern era to do so. In the 108 previous World Series, only eight Cardinals have played in as many as four World Series with the franchise, and Molina is the first to do it since 1946, when Stan Musial and the Swifties defeated, yes, Boston in seven games.

Told about the imminent distinction, Molina recalled when it started, in 2004.

"I feel blessed," Molina said in the Cardinals dugout after a workout this week at Busch Stadium. "When I came up in '04, I was one of the young guys and I see so many of these guys, like Albert Pujols, Matheny, Larry Walker and Woody Williams there — all winners. They're winners. They taught me that this is what it's about. You don't play this game just to play it. You don't play this game just to put up the numbers. You play it to win, to win championships. The way they taught me that year was the beginning. That has been the key for me."

The Cardinals held a brief batting practice Monday afternoon at Busch before taking a charter to Boston for media obligations and a workout today at Fenway Park. Weather permitting, Game 1 of the World Series between baseball's two 97-win teams will start at 7:07 p.m. (St. Louis time) Wednesday, and three outs later Molina will call Adam Wainwright's first pitch. This will be the Cardinals' fourth visit to the World Series in 10 years — their fourth since Molina's rookie year — twice as many as any other team in baseball, save for their opponent. The Red Sox are playing in their third since 2004.

Less than a handful of players remain from that 2004 Series on both sides of the diamond. David Ortiz was there for Boston. Matheny, Chris Carpenter and Molina remain of the players there for the Cardinals. Like Molina, Carpenter has been with the Cardinals for the past four National League pennant-winning clubs, but because of injuries Carpenter has

Cardinals vs. Houston Astros. Molina and Steve Kline.

Cardinals vs. New York Mets. Molina and Albert Pujols.

only pitched in two World Series. Pujols appeared in three. Wainwright is about to be a part of his third, the second in which he'll pitch.

The championship eras of Cardinals baseball all cluster around similar cores, like Bob Gibson's El Birdos and their three World Series in the 1960s or Ozzie Smith's three trips in the 1980s. The rare groups, like Frankie Frisch's teams and Musial's Swifties, have won four pennants. Four of the nine four-timers are in the Hall of Fame.

That was the thought general manager John Mozeliak had on a recent flight.

He saw where Molina's ascension could lead.

"The trajectory that his career is on could end up in Cooperstown," Mozeliak said Monday. "You think about his evolution as a major-league player and he's being talked about with the names of some of the

Cardinals vs. Milwaukee Brewers. Molina and Jason Motte.

greatest players to ever catch. Yadi's pace may surpass them all."

Molina, who was 22 when he made his World Series debut, had the championship before he had the production that supports such thoughts. A glove-first catcher at the beginning of his career, Molina turned into an offensive force in October 2006 and an MVP candidate in 2012. He and Pittsburgh's Andrew McCutchen are positioned as the two MVP contenders this season.

Molina's career-high .319 average led the Cardinals in hitting for the second consecutive year, and Molina's 44 doubles are the second-highest single-season total for a catcher in more than 100 years. Despite spending time on the disabled list with a knee injury, Molina still led the NL in innings behind the plate, 37 more than the next-closest catcher. He also shepherded the Cardinals' cavalcade of rookie pitchers, and did so with a career-low 3.16 ERA when he was behind the plate.

"His baseball IQ is off the charts," Mozeliak said. "He has the ability to lead young pitchers — or any pitchers for that matter. When you look at our glue, he's become it."

So much attention this October, locally and nationally, has focused on the "Cardinal Way," the philosophy and the actual handbook that has offered the blueprint for a self-sustaining franchise and its style of play. Musial gets name-dropped. Dave Duncan and Tony La Russa credited. George Kissell praised. Red Schoendienst celebrated. Molina embodies another chapter in the Cardinal Way, the one authored by Dave Ricketts, the club's longtime catching coach who died in 2008. Molina has called him a father figure. Molina was a pupil of Ricketts and an apprentice of Ricketts' disciple Matheny. He can still recite lessons from Ricketts.

In that way, Molina offers a quality control for the Cardinals, the one conducting everything on the field, from defensive positioning to pitch location. He has followed the word that Matheny uses in the Cardinal Way handbook as one of the 16 characteristics every catcher must have: "selflessness."

Pitcher first.

Team first.

October first.

"Some players are great catchers but didn't have the opportunity that I have had being in the World Series. I know that," Molina said. "It's about being a part of a good team. I don't really care about numbers. I want to see them because if you've got the numbers you're helping the team. There's more to it. If I can move the runner over, get the runner over with a ground ball to second — that's the playoffs. It's about finding ways to win. That's how I want to help the team. That's what the playoffs are about."

Molina has long defined himself by what happens at this time of year. In his first start, he announced his presence by standing up and confronting Manny Ramirez at the plate. Ortiz was on the on-deck circle, and Molina wanted to send a message about how he wouldn't tolerate stealing signs. Two years later, Molina found redemption

in October. Irritated by the .216 average he had in 2006, Molina led the majors with 19 hits in the postseason, including the home run that put the Cardinals ahead in Game 7 of the National League championship series.

In three World Series trips, he's hit .341, higher than any of the other four-timers.

He has embraced the Cardinals' notion that they are defined by the postseason. It's not just how he thinks. It's how he inks. The World Series trophy tattoo he has covers his right biceps and is exponentially larger than the Gold Gloves and stars he has on the other arm.

Only 31 and ready for his fourth World Series, he may run out of room.

"Four times is an impressive feat, definitely adding to his legacy," Matheny said. "It's no coincidence. Championship-caliber players like him are the ones who always have a way of finding championship-level opportunities." ∎

Cardinals vs. Los Angeles Dodgers. Molina and Trevor Rosenthal.

NO SECRET FOR MOLINA, JUST WORK

By Bernie Miklasz
March 6, 2014

JUPITER, Fla. — Shelby Miller has a theory on Yadier Molina's brilliance as a catcher. Sure, Molina has abundant talent like the quick arm he uses as a whip to strike down base-stealing thieves. He's devoted to preparation and has a legendary work ethic. Intelligence? Well, Molina's mind is even more imposing than his arm. But there's something else …

What's the secret?

When you watch a Cardinals game on TV this season, and the camera zooms in for a view from above center field, follow Molina's eyes. He'll be looking up. His head will cock slightly to the side. His eyes — bright and visible — will be taking a furtive glance at the hitter.

"It's almost like he can look right into a hitter's soul," Miller said Wednesday after making his first spring start. "And Yadier knows what to do with that. He stares at the hitter, and you can see him thinking. 'What pitch can't you hit right now.' And if he calls the pitch, then you know that's got to be the one.

You throw it, and it works. He's thinking the entire game. He's aware of everything that's going on.

"I would say he's the smartest player in the game."

When Miller's observation was relayed to Molina, baseball's best catcher laughed. That's because Miller's comment reminded Yadi of an exchange he had with Arizona's Martin Prado during last year's World Baseball Classic.

Molina was catching for his native Puerto Rico. And when Prado, competing for Venezuela, stepped into the batter's box, Molina's eyes would turn into laser beams. Prado felt it. He was distressed.

"What Shelby said was funny, because Prado told me the same thing during the World Classic," Molina said. "Every time he was up he said, 'Don't look at me, stop looking at me, don't try to read me, don't read my mind.' It is funny."

Only to a point.

There are no secrets.

"It comes with preparation you do before the game," Molina said. "I spend so many hours watching the video of the other team's starting lineup, seeing what I can learn. I'm just doing my job."

So Molina is not looking into a hitter's soul.

"I don't think so," he said, laughing. "It's the work. The preparation."

Molina is getting ready for his 11th season as a Cardinal, and the 10th as the full-time starter. Molina was a young catcher of 21 when he made his debut as Mike Matheny's backup for the 2004 Cardinals, who won 105 games and the NL pennant.

In this balmy Florida spring of 2014, Molina is 31 and the most respected catcher in the game. And he's already among the most acclaimed catchers in baseball history.

Molina has won the Gold Glove for defense for six consecutive years, he's been chosen to play in the All-Star Game for five years running, and he's caught more innings than anyone except A.J. Pierzynski since 2004.

Molina's catcher ERA of 3.71 ranks No. 1 and is well below MLB's overall ERA of 4.20 since 2004. His work with young pitchers is a valuable element in their success; last October the Cardinals set a major-league record for most innings pitched by rookies in a postseason. And the baby birds did great.

Molina's throw-out rate of 44.5 percent since he came to St. Louis in 2004 is the best among big-league catchers. That's more than 13 percentage points higher than the next catcher on the list and is 17 points higher than the industry standard over that time.

Oh … and in his spare time, Molina studies more game video than an NFL coach, runs strategy meetings, scripts detailed scouting reports, maps the daily plan of attack for every Cardinals pitcher, calls every pitch, adjusts his fielders' positioning, makes visits to the mound, finesses the strike zone by framing pitches, goes to the mound to calm young pitchers, shouts instructions and encouragement to veteran pitchers.

And if that isn't enough, over the past three seasons Molina has turned into quite a hitter, with a .313 average, .361 on-base percentage, .481 slugging percentage — and an average of 16 homers, 35 doubles and 74 RBIs per season.

That's all very nice, but this is what pleases Molina the most: In his 10 seasons with St. Louis the Cardinals have made the postseason seven times, winning four NL pennants and two World Series. Molina has caught 80 postseason games in his career; only retired Yankees catcher Jorge Posada (119) had more.

Ask him about possibly being voted into the Baseball Hall of Fame. Ask him about winning a league MVP award after finishing fourth and third, respectively, in the voting the last two seasons. Ask him about the Gold Gloves, or any individual accolades.

Not interested.

"It's hard to get into the Hall of Fame. For me, I don't like to think about it," Molina said. "For me, this game is so hard, that if you start thinking about awards, you're going to get caught up and lose focus. When I wake up each day, I just want to win that day's game, and help the team any way I can. And then I want to do the same thing next day. A good year for me is our team getting to the World Series and winning it."

St. Louis Cardinals catcher Yadier Molina works a bunting drill at the Cardinals spring training complex at Roger Dean Stadium in Jupiter, Fla.

This is what drives Molina. This is why he works so hard. For a 7 o'clock game, he arrives at the ballpark by 1 p.m. and invests three or four hours scanning video of that night's opposing hitters to plan a strategy. He passes along his scouting insights to coaches and pitchers.

Molina sometimes takes his work home with him after games. He's married and has two children, but after the house turns quiet, and everyone is sleeping, a restless catcher is stirring.

"I don't sleep that well, so whenever I'm in bed I like to study there too if I have to," Molina said. "It's all about the work. There are no shortcuts. I care. I care about winning. I care about my pitchers. I care about my team. So if I care, I need to work. So that means go to the video, and study, and be prepared."

Molina also wants to win for Cardinals fans. He made it a point to mention that when he cited the factors that motivate him to give his best ... and to be the best. And the fans were a reason he signed a five-year, $75 million contract that runs through 2017.

Molina surely could have cashed in for more money by taking his name, and all-around game, to the free agent market.

"Maybe, but you want to be at a place where you can be happy with your family," Molina said. "And every time I play a game in St. Louis, I'm happy. The last 10 years have been truly amazing. The way the fans treat me, even when I was a young player, doing bad, they treated me right. I mean, just for that I decided to stay here.

"For me it's nothing better than being a Cardinal and being in that city. For me it's as special as it can be. I am having fun there. I love the organization, the team that we have, and the effort they put in every year to try to win. The fans show up for every game, and give you all of the support you could ask for. I don't think there's any place like this."

No, Molina really can't really look into the soul of the hitter.

But if you want to see the soul of the Cardinals, then look behind home plate, the special place where Yadier Molina works. ∎

MOLINA SECURES STATUS AS CARDINALS LEGEND

By Benjamin Hochman
April 3, 2017

Benjamin Molina Sr. sculpted him, the best of the brothers, who redefined how to play a baseball position, Ozzie-esque. And now, with Sunday's news of a new contract until 2020, the vision of Yadier Molina is now one that must be sculpted again.

"I just hope I stay alive long enough," said Harry Weber, 74, the man who sculpted most of the statues outside Busch Stadium. "He's absolutely amazing."

Yadi is a legend already, and his legend continues, into 2017 and likely into his 17th year in the majors, the 2020 season, which could be the last of an epic Cardinals career — one worthy of a number on the outfield wall and a statue on Clark.

"In an era where sometimes people say they're cheering for uniforms, because the personnel changes are so rapid and so thorough, Yadier represents something that is a lasting Cardinal value," Weber said. "He started there, he's identified with the team, he's already a team legend.

"He's a Cardinal in the same vein that Musial was and Schoendienst was and Gibson was. That happened a lot more often in the '40s, '50s, '60s and '70s — it doesn't happen very often now. But it sure does in Yadier's case."

That's why this contract is so important. It affirms that Yadi will be a Jeter. A classic single-digited, single-teamed, multi-championed icon, forever bronzed but with a glove of gold. It just feels right. Oh, and it's a pretty good investment, too. Yadi isn't done. Will he be a star in 2020? Hard to say. Would he have earned $20 million AAV on the open market this winter? Probably not. But watching him this spring, he doesn't look 34 out there.

And this contract, right here, captures why a lucrative TV deal makes the rich get richer, because it gives a team a cushion to take a potential risk, if the team even sees it as one.

"Today's not about a sun-setting career," general manager John Mozeliak said. "... And to me this is much more than what he's done: What it means to me is what he's going to do. In a way, today is just the next chapter in our future. We believe he can compete at the highest level, and we still feel that Yadi is one of the greatest catchers in the game. He's in great shape, he trains hard, he eats well and he knows what's important not only about today but tomorrow. ...

"He is someone we still expect to be an elite performer."

In a game tethered to numbers, the numbers don't properly capture the importance of Yadier Benjamin Molina. That's what's so cool about Yadi, because his numbers actually have been very good at times. Even some fancy sabermetrics can't quantify Molina's impact. Since 2004, when he snatched the job from the man who's now his manager, he's made pitchers better, batters worse and baserunners bait.

"He has set the standard for defensive excellence during this generation," Cardinals Chairman Bill DeWitt Jr. said. "There is no question, he is without equal in managing a pitching staff."

Yadi is fascinating because he epitomizes the seriousness of playing the game right and hard; yet his most-memorable moments have him grinning that boyish grin — flying into the arms of Adam Wainwright, or Jason Motte, or floating around the bases at Shea. And it's that mix of personas that make him so beloved, and to be a ballplayer beloved in St. Louis, my word, it must be bliss. Yadier Molina could sneeze in St. Louis and earn applause.

"I didn't want to go anywhere else," Yadi said Sunday, as his family stood nearby during the contract announcement. He admitted that he wasn't afraid to test free agency this winter, but that "This is the right place to be. … This is a winning organization, and I'm a winning player. I see myself doing good stuff from now on, especially winning another World Series, one or two more, three, four? That's my idea."

The day will come.

It could be in three years. Four years. Shoot, six?

But there will be a day when smart baseball men decide that Yadier Molina isn't the Cardinals' best option at catcher.

Maybe, by then, the "Yadi-heir" won't be Carson Kelly anymore. Man, remember him? Suddenly, this doesn't sound like a simple transition of power behind the plate. The kid catcher is heralded as the best in the minors, "and had this deal not worked out, maybe there would've been different dynamics there," Mozeliak said. "But he's still growing as a catcher and a player, and now he can learn from one of the best."

But whenever that fateful day arrives for Yadi, Sunday's contract signing means it will probably be as a St. Louis Cardinal.

When Yadi was offered the contract, Bengie Molina Jr. received a call while at home in Arizona.

"Yadi said, 'Hey man, we've got a deal, what do you think?'" Bengie Jr. recalled Sunday, as the Molina family filed into the press conference room. "And I said, 'What the hell do you think I think? Heck yeah! This is your chance to finish your career in your city.'

"It's so cool man. You don't see it that often."

With a new $60-million deal to keep him in St. Louis through 2020, Yadier Molina takes batting practice before the start of Sunday's opener against the Cubs.

A woman walked up to Bengie while holding a young boy.

"This is the next first rounder!" Bengie said. "We need to wait 17 years though!"

I wasn't sure if it was his son or perhaps Yadi's. Then, on cue, the boy smiled and there was no question. It was Yadier's son, Daniel Benjamin Molina, flashing the smile that lights up St. Louis. ∎

WHAT A GROOVY FELINE

Molina's grand slam follows cat's impromptu appearance

By Derrick Goold
August 10, 2017

There for a brief moment, before rally cat came into their lives, Yadier Molina paused at the plate, stood tall, and pointed his bat toward left field, appearing as if he were calling his shot.

He wasn't.

Something more dramatic was about to happen.

Molina was one of the first to spot the latest cute critter to run onto the Busch Stadium field and into Cardinals lore. With the bases loaded, Kansas City up by a run, and Molina ahead in the count, a dark gray kitten with lynx-like ears loped toward the infield and then darted out to center. Once the cat had taken a piece of the grounds crew member's finger and still been corralled, the game resumed. Molina put the next pitch where he once appeared to be pointing — into the left-field seats. El Gato Slam.

The catcher's fifth career grand slam sent the Cardinals to an 8-5 victory against the Royals and the kitten into legend.

"I'm not a cat person," manager Mike Matheny said. "But I sure like that one."

The rally delivered the Cardinals' fifth consecutive victory and put them within reach of the division leaders. Coupled with the Cubs' loss in San Francisco, the Cardinals' win put them 1½ games back in the National League Central, the closest they've been in the division race since June 13. The last time the Cardinals (58-56) were within a game of the division leader was also the last time they were two games better than .500, on May 27.

The Cardinals had been teasing, teasing, teasing a breakout inning throughout the game, though each

Cardinals catcher Yadier Molina gestures to a small cat that made its way past Royals center fielder Lorenzo Cain.

time the inning unraveled into a familiar yarn. Three times, Molina came to the plate with a runner in scoring position before his grand slam, and he flied out twice and grounded out once. He missed on chances to bring home a tying run and an insurance run, but the Cardinals' newly rejuvenated offense found a way to give him a fourth chance. KC reliever Brandon Maurer didn't retire either of the two batters he faced. Greg Garcia singled, and Matt Carpenter walked. Peter Moylan entered and retired two batters, though an error allowed both Garcia and Carpenter to advance 90 feet.

The Royals opted to intentionally walk Dexter Fowler and dare Molina with the bases loaded. Molina took a slider for a ball, and then saw the cat.

"I thought it was a streaker on the field, to be honest," Matheny said.

"You never expect animals," Molina said. "The catcher (Cam Gallagher) told me, 'You ever seen something like that before?' I said, 'Not with a cat, but with a squirrel, yes.'"

If ever Molina looks at his 2011 World Series ring he can still see the squirrel. Such a celebrated presence from the Cardinals' 2011 championship run, the squirrel that interrupted Skip Schumaker's at-bat in the

playoffs quickly became an icon, launching T-shirts, cheers, and even a mascot for a local children's hospital. Ownership included a silhouette of "Rally Squirrel" on the ring. So, yes, Molina has seen this before. Once the cat crossed their path, the Royals never had a chance.

Molina drove Moylan's next pitch for his 14th homer of the season.

The cat was captured in center field by Lucas Hackmann, a member of the grounds crew. The cat appeared to bite Hackmann on the finger, and a photo of him appeared later on social media showing a bandaged finger. Hackman was taken to Barnes-Jewish Hospital for treatment and possible shots. The cat's whereabouts were the stuff of legend. A Busch Stadium official said there were "so many different stories that I can't even speculate." The Cardinals did not have possession of the cat at game's end, though they were not sure if it was left with the Humane Society of Missouri or some other group or person. Matheny said he was told by security that someone had already "claimed the cat."

It's not clear if the cat was just a stray, trying to find its way, and scurrying around Busch Stadium hoping for direction.

Yadier Molina is congratulated by Dexter Fowler after hitting a grand slam in the sixth inning Wednesday night against the Royals.

Like, you know, a metaphor.

For most of the season the Cardinals had been given life after life in the division race because of the mishaps above them in the standings. The Cardinals returned home to Busch after a road trip that saw them take control of their ability to contend. The Cardinals tied a club record by scoring at least 10 runs in three consecutive games, and that offense nourished the team's return to .500. The Cardinals shed the meandering look they've had for so long, and on Wednesday showed the new bite that they have. Mike Leake's early struggles left them down 3-0 by the middle of the second inning. They answered with four unanswered runs, including Jose Martinez's solo homer for a lead.

When Leake allowed a two-run homer that shifted the game back to KC, the Cardinals remained on the prowl for runs, a persistence they haven't showed much this season.

"I'd be lying to you if I didn't say there were times this year when we you get down three and you don't feel real good about coming back," Carpenter said. "You don't feel that right now. We got down 3-0 in a hurry and I can promise you there wasn't a guy in that dugout who not only was thinking but knew we were going to score some runs. And we did."

Added Matheny: "You just think the next guy is going to do it because you've recently seen the next guy do it. It's one of those things you keep building on."

To nibble into the Royals' three-run lead, the Cardinals got frisky against starter Trevor Cahill. Kolten Wong took a walk, stole second, and then scored on Leake's safety squeeze in the second. In the third, Fowler drew a walk, stole second, and was able to score on Jedd Gyorko's single. While Leake was allowing the Royals five runs on 11 hits in his five innings, the Cardinals were able to chase Cahill in the third.

When Fowler walked to load the bases for Molina, the Cardinals did in the game what they're now in position to do in the division.

They pounced.

"There were too many guys in this clubhouse who weren't performing to their career norms," Carpenter said. "When you have that many guys underachieving individually and collectively, that's not where we want to be. You've got to believe eventually that's going to change. It looks like it's happening all at the same time. Which has a chance to be special." ■

LOOK WHAT THE CAT DRAGGED IN — HOPE

By Benjamin Hochman • August 10, 2017

Somewhere in St. Louis, in the John Burroughs of burrows, the Rally Squirrel retired to a leisurely life of high-end acorns … when Wednesday he heard the news of his purring peer.

"Ran on the field during a Cards game?" the Rally Squirrel must have thought. "Copy cat."

The year the Rally Squirrel delayed a postseason at-bat at Busch, the Cards won the World Series. And on Wednesday, in the midst of a tight division race, a cat ran on the field, interrupting the Cards-Royals game. He became #RallyCat.

After local-folk-hero-to-be Lucas Hackmann scooped up the cat in center field, Yadier Molina drilled the next pitch for a go-ahead grand slam.

"I knew before the cat ran on the field, just seeing Yadi walk up to the plate, I felt good about our chances," the Cards' Matt Carpenter said after the 8-5 win. "And then I saw the cat, and I knew something special was about to happen."

Look, it's still going to be tough to knock off the Cubs, even if they can't beat the Giants (and even if their stud catcher is injured). And the '17 Cards are underachieving from an offensive standpoint (considering that two guys who were supposed to be key producers are on the Memphis Redbirds now).

But Wednesday's win sure was fun. And talk about galvanizing a team and city — all thanks to a stray cat strut.

(Someone suggested on Twitter that people have been known to bring cats in purses to Busch Stadium, to which local reporter Brian Stull responded: "And keep it locked in there for six innings?").

I liked this Tweet from Adam Butz (@DrButz): "Such a pedestrian, ho-hum season thus far. Cat runs across the field — and now I'm convinced we are winning it all! #rallycat #STLCards."

In baseball, we love the magic of the random. The peculiar, inexplicable intrusion of, say, weather or even an animal. It's like sport is this impenetrable vacuum, and the athletes are unwaveringly focused on their craft … until a cat somehow shows up and has the players laughing uproariously.

And so, in the matter of moments, Rally Cat joined the litany of cats in the Cards' litter, including Andres "Big Cat" Galarraga, Harry "The Cat" Brecheen, Harvey "Kitten" Haddix and Jim "Kitty" Kaat. Famed Fox Sports Midwest reporter Jim Hayes goes by "The Cat."

And of course, this is the proud franchise of the likes of Pawsie Smith, Tommy Purr, the aforementioned Yadi Meowlina and Hard Hittin' Mark Kitten. ∎

A Busch Stadium grounds keeper retrieves a small cat that ran across the outfield past Kansas City Royals center fielder Lorenzo Cain in the sixth inning.

MOLINA GOES ON MISSION OF MERCY

With food, water and hugs, Molina delivers help to Puerto Rico

By Derrick Goold
October 18, 2017

ST. LOUIS — A short drive from where Yadier Molina grew up in Vega Alta, Puerto Rico, and into the Mavilla neighborhood, the Cardinals catcher stood atop a blacktop road surrounded by stripped-clean and snapped trees and covered with a message that gave words to the reason he came home.

"AYUDA," it listed. "AGUA. ALIMENTO."

Translated it asked for "help," "water," and "food."

Written atop, "SOS."

No translation needed.

Cardinals catcher Yadier Molina, as part of his work with Fundacion 4, delivers goods such as water and food to residents of his hometown in Puerto Rico. Molina visited in person with supplies to help people recover from the damage left by Hurricane Maria.

The road and the request scrawled along it are clear in a photo that Molina posted last week on his Instagram page. In it, Molina, wearing a St. Louis Blues T-shirt, stands beside residents as part of his visit to Puerto Rico to do exactly what was asked — bring food, water and help to an area still recovering from the damage of Hurricane Maria.

Molina, along with his older brother Jose and wife Wanda, visited the area around Vega Alta in the past week and went door to door with supplies, according to a description provided by Evelyn Guadalupe, a spokesman for Molina's Fundacion 4.

Molina traveled the area without journalists so he could knock on the doors and spend time with neighbors, many of whom are still without power and some of whom were already in what he has described as an underprivileged area.

He chronicled the visits on Instagram and in photos provided by his foundation. In them, Molina is delivering water, dry goods and many embraces. In one photo, Molina is clutching hands with a neighbor and in the background stand statues of him and his two brothers, all three of whom played catcher in the major leagues. Molina's foundation delivered trucks loaded with ice as well as water and other provisions. In one video Molina shared, palettes were stacked with water bottles 12 deep and six bottles high.

A month after Hurricane Maria tore through Puerto Rico, many of the 3.4 million U.S. citizens living there still lack power, clean water and basic supplies. Communication is limited or nonexistent across the island. Reports from this past weekend said 1.2 million residents do not have potable water, and Puerto Rico's electric power authority said 85 percent of the island does not have power. Scores of Americans remain unaccounted for and this past weekend the death toll rose, nearing 50.

The island, its crippled infrastructure and its recovery have become a quagmire for President Donald Trump, who has used Twitter to engage in spats with officials or question the extent of help the federal government can provide. He wrote on Twitter that the grid and infrastructure were a "disaster"

before the hurricane and that federal relief could not go on "forever." This past week, Congress passed relief funding.

In the closing days of the Cardinals' season, as he recovered from post-concussion symptoms, Molina declined to wade into the politics of Puerto Rico's recovery.

He stressed that his role should be "helping as many people as possible."

"I am going to go to help," he said.

Two days after the Cardinals' season ended, Molina did that. After stopping in Florida to help organize goods, Molina and his wife traveled to Puerto Rico to handle the deliveries in person. According to Guadalupe's description, the foundation had five trucks "loaded with provisions." Shortly after Hurricane Maria and its eye wall passed near Molina's hometown of Vega Alta, the catcher started a GoFundMe account that raised more than $155,000. Molina said that money would go to purchase the supplies brought to the towns and neighborhoods around Vega Alta.

Before leaving St. Louis, Molina said he would add to the fund with a personal donation. He did not disclose how much. Several teammates, including Kolten Wong and Tommy Pham, also provided financial support for Molina's efforts.

Molina's group visited at least four towns during the humanitarian trip, which ended Sunday.

Two of the towns have welcomed Molina before as he makes annual trips in with turkeys that he gives families for Thanksgiving dinner as part of Fundacion 4's work. Yadier and Wanda Molina founded their charitable organization in 2010.

He has also hosted Christmas parties in the neighborhoods.

In December, Molina will return to Puerto Rico to host the second annual Yadier Molina Home Run Derby & Celebrity Softball Game. The event will be at San Juan, Puerto Rico's Hiram Bithorn Stadium, and Molina's foundation announced this week that proceeds will benefit organizations that are helping residents recover from Hurricane Maria damage.

In the "SOS" photo, which Molina shared on Instagram on Thursday, the Cardinals catcher shares the frame with as many as nine children and friends who traveled with him from home to home to deliver items. The popular social media site allows people to tap a heart icon if they "like" the photo, and as of Tuesday morning more than 9,950 people had.

One was Carlos Beltran.

"I have friends and family over there and things are not getting better," Beltran told the New York Post.

The former Cardinals outfielder is currently playing for Houston in the American League championship series while also watching and helping his homeland's recovery. "For the first week and a half, I couldn't sleep. I was going crazy. I didn't hear from my family for a week. Everyone is in the same boat, all different classes. You can have money, but if you don't have food to buy, then you don't have anything. The situation is critical.

"If they want it to disappear," Beltran told the paper, "then Puerto Rico is going to disappear." ∎

Cardinals catcher Yadier Molina, wearing a St. Louis Blues shirt, greets a neighbor in his hometown of Vega Alta, Puerto Rico. Statues of Molina and his brothers, who also played in the major leagues, are in the background. Molina traveled to Puerto Rico with supplies to help residents who are still recovering from the damage left by Hurricane Maria.

'HELLO, YADIER MOLINA. I'M ADAM WAINWRIGHT. YOU NEW AROUND HERE?'

By Derrick Goold
February 17, 2018

JUPITER, Fla. — A tradition many years in the making that only started a few years ago, Cardinals starter Adam Wainwright introduced himself to catcher Yadier Molina on Saturday morning before they did something they have, famously, more than a hundred times over.

"Hello," Wainwright said, extending a hand. "I'm Adam Wainwright. You new around here?"

Molina, under his mask, responded.

He asked what Wainwright likes to throw.

"I'm a power guy," the starter said, with a grin.

On the fourth day of official workouts, Wainwright threw his second side session of spring, and this time Molina caught him for the first time in 2018. Molina got his first bullpen sessions in Friday with Carlos Martinez, and on Saturday he drew Wainwright and newcomer Bud Norris as his assignments.

No pitcher-catcher battery in Cardinals history have had more time together than Molina and Wainwright, who surpassed Bob Gibson and Tim McCarver more than a year ago and still have at least another year together. They've been together in the majors since 2006, and they've been in the same spring training for two years before that. Wainwright is signed through the end of this season, and Molina is in the first year of a three-year extension he signed last spring.

They have grown up together in the Cardinals organization, they have won together in the Cardinals organization, and they are forever linked together in the Cardinals organization.

They will stand on opening day in the distant future wearing red blazers together at whatever stadium the Cardinals call home.

"He's like my brother," Molina said after the day's workout. "I want him to feel good. I want him to be excited for what he can do. This is part of the family. I need to see him happy."

Molina remained animated throughout the throw with Wainwright as he worked through the progression of about 20 to 25 pitches. Wainwright was working on some of his arm angles, and there was a video camera capturing his throws for review later. Even before the start of Saturday's workouts, Molina said he was eager to see Wainwright throw, and it's clear that the Cardinals' Gold Glove catcher sees

Wainwright's return from injury and from a difficult year as a team effort, something they want as much for the righthander as he does.

Molina shouted encouragement about how the changeup faded to the edge of the plate or how the fastball found his target.

Toward the end of Wainwright's session, he wanted to work through at-bats with Molina keeping count. Wainwright got ahead, 0-1, with a fastball. He hooked a slider that wasn't close to the strike zone for 1-1. Molina shouted to him that it was still 0-1. The catcher was essentially offering a mulligan for the pitch and telling Wainwright to try again.

Wainwright said, "1-1."

So, 1-1, it was.

The righthander missed with two more pitches to fall behind the count 3-1 with three consecutive balls. Molina called for a changeup, and Wainwright put it on the edge of the plate to run the count full. With his next-to-last pitch of the session and pitching coach Mike Maddux positioned nearby, Wainwright and Molina went to the pitch they so often have in a bind.

Wainwright spun a curveball that on the way toward the strike zone dropped out of it and into the dirt just behind the plate.

Molina blocked it, and made the call.

"Strike out," he said. "That's a strike out."

St. Louis Cardinals catcher Yadier Molina talks with pitcher Adam Wainwright during St. Louis Cardinals spring training on Friday, Feb. 16, 2018, in Jupiter, Fla.

In the clubhouse after the workout Saturday, Molina tugged on his shoes and talked about that sequence of pitches and the finish.

"That's him. That's him," the catcher said. "I'm happy for him."

For all pitchers who threw Saturday this was their second time through the side sessions. There will be a third time through for some as they build up pitch count, and on Monday a group of the pitchers will launch right into facing hitters in live batting practice sessions. Cardinals officials, such as manager Mike Matheny and John Mozeliak, have both said it's important to fight the temptation of judging Wainwright on his first bullpen session (or his second), on his first time facing hitters, or even on his first appearance in games.

Wainwright, however, has sought that level of scrutiny, suggesting that he's going into this spring like he had to years ago, when he really did have to introduce himself to his catcher.

At the end of their reunion Saturday, Molina and Wainwright met in the middle and talked through the action the catch saw on his pitches and the consistency of the angles that Wainwright's arm took.

Wainwright jogged away to his next station, but not before a pat.

"Good to see you again," he told his catcher. ∎

The Cardinals Adam Wainwright and catcher Yadier Molina celebrate the last out and winning of Game 5 Friday and the World Series between the St. Louis Cardinals and the Detroit Tigers at Busch Stadium in St. Louis.

HIGHWAY TO COOPERSTOWN?

Another All-Star Game appearance adds to Molina's increasing résumé

By Derrick Goold
July 17, 2018

WASHINGTON — A backstop Yadier Molina emulated as a boy, Sandy Alomar Jr., bent the knees that sometimes betrayed him as a catcher, took a seat, and tried to describe the ways Molina has revolutionized their position to increase his durability.

He pantomimed how Molina sometimes gloves bouncers like an infielder to get in a better position to throw, how Molina waits to drop to his knees to avoid telegraphing a curveball and to protect the joints, and how his stance doesn't give away his pitch call. Alomar, during a recent visit to Busch Stadium, tried to think of other catchers who were similar.

When he thought of someone, he grinned.

Enter the "Dragon."

"Do you know Bruce Lee?" the Cleveland coach asked. "He went to every style of martial arts and tried to find one that fit him best and decided, 'No, I'll create my own style.' Who does that? Yadier Molina does that. He created his own style of catching. I see Yadi and I see a different evolution of catching. The way he's catching. The stances. For him, catching — it's like art. He has taken it to a different level.

"He stands now with the legends," Alomar concluded. "It's Johnny Bench, Pudge Rodriguez, and you put him with those guys."

At 36, the Cardinals catcher has become a marvel for his peers as he moves into the autumn of his career and starts surpassing the career feats of giants at his position.

Earlier this season, Molina moved past Bench in innings caught (now 14,894). Molina's 1,778 games caught for one major-league team is another record set this season, and in the next month he'll move into seventh place in regular-season and postseason games started at catcher, moving past Benito Santiago's 1,823.

All of this has stoked the conversation about whether Molina, at career's end, will be ushered to Cooperstown, N.Y.

The 89th All-Star Game on Tuesday night brings with it another honor for Molina. He is the only member of either league's roster with more than seven All-Star selections. He has nine.

This year's honor, which came despite missing a month because of a violent injury to his groin, makes him one of 11 players to have at least nine All-Star

Cardinals catcher Yadier Molina has been selected for his ninth All-Star Game, and is a reserve for the NL.

games, win eight Gold Glove awards and have two top-five MVP voting finishes. Fellow Puerto Rican Roberto Clemente is one, Bench is the only other catcher, and nine of the other 10 are in the National Baseball Hall of Fame. Barry Bonds is not.

'THAT'S A HALL OF FAMER'

"For what my two cents are worth, the Hall of Fame is about a celebration of the best players and the longevity in the game of the best players," said Giants catcher and former MVP Buster Posey. "We've got all these fancy stats now on who is and who isn't, but I think really, anybody who has been around the game, when they hear the name Yadier Molina they think, 'That's a Hall of Famer.' That's my logic. But I'm not objective at all."

Several years ago, Bench told the Post-Dispatch that Molina was on the highway to Cooperstown and suggested all he needed was to burnish his baseball card with counting stats and trophies.

Another title, or two.

A 10th Gold Glove.

Hits. Homers. The like.

Last weekend Molina secured his spot with the second-most starts in a day game after night game for a catcher. (He has 276.) His next homer will tie him with Bill White's 140 for 14th in Cardinals history. He's 207 hits shy of becoming the 11th catcher with

2,000, and two more seasons of 130 hits will vault him into the top seven.

Molina has said he intends to retire when his current contract expires at the end of 2020.

A close friend said Monday that's not a given, and if Molina's healthy he'll be lobbied to play one more year "as a victory lap."

Longevity could sweeten some of the stats that are a drag on his candidacy, such as the Wins Above Replacement camp or bulk voters who like mounting counting stats.

Many peers say the numbers can't quantify Molina.

On Monday at Nationals Park, Reds first baseman Joey Votto smiled when asked if all his at-bats against the division rival aren't so much against the pitcher but vs. Molina.

"Oh yeah," Votto said. "He's just got a sense. I don't feel like I see a lot of head shakes from the pitchers. I play the guessing game a little bit with pitchers, and I'm really competing with him. And I'm guessing wrong all the time. It's like he can sniff out, he can sense where any hitter is looking or what they're attempting. It's something that I don't think you can measure. That seems like an intangible. But he has it. He's gotten better.

"I wonder if in the future (there will be that stat)," Votto added. "I hope that baseball appreciates what they have in him."

'THIS GUY IS THE BEST'

For one, consider the curse word.

In his office at Chase Field earlier this month, Arizona Diamondbacks manager Torey Lovullo discussed the importance of apologizing in person to Molina for what he said on the field earlier this season.

During an argument with an umpire, Lovullo used a disparaging term to describe Molina, one that caused Molina to charge him. Lovullo's intent was actually to compliment Molina — suggesting he didn't need the ump's help stealing strikes. He's that good.

"I was really, aggressively — and not at all in the way I meant — saying this guy is the best," Lovullo said. "There is zero glove movement. It's like natural. It changes games. It's fun to watch because baseball people appreciate greatness. He makes greatness look easy."

For two, consider the Brazilian.

Cleveland catcher Yan Gomes, an All-Star, visited Busch this season and described what he felt as he stepped up to the batter's box.

"I'm a big fan and trying not to go giggly on him," Gomes said. "In a way, you just want to look at him and tell him, 'It's a great honor to share a field with you.' I can always said I did that. He is the face of catching. He's the guy in several years — you know how they talk about Yogi Berra? Yeah, Molina is that guy."

For three, consider the countrymen.

Two of the most energizing and charismatic players in Tuesday's night's game will be Cleveland shortstop Francisco Lindor and Cubs second baseman Javy Baez. They shared a clubhouse with Molina in the World Baseball Classic and remain on a Team Puerto Rico text chain in which players talk to each other. They each grew up idolizing the Molina Brothers, Bengie, Jose, and youngest brother Yadier.

"Who didn't look up to him?" Lindor asked. "He's a born winner. He wins everywhere he goes. He is a Hall of Famer. Whether that's in Puerto Rico or that's with the Cardinals Hall of Fame or it's in the National Baseball Hall of Fame. He's already a legend."

Molina's seat for Monday's media scrum at Nationals Park was in the back of the room. Fitting, from there he could do what he does professionally: read the opposition.

He also could celebrate the stars that have started to sparkle all around him. Six members, including Molina, from Team Puerto Rico are at the All-Star Game. Only Molina is older than 25. That means the other five weren't yet teenagers when he debuted in 2004. They grew up as he grew into an icon of their island.

"The father figure?" Molina asked. "That makes me old."

It means he's been able to do what Alomar said he's done as well as anyone: To be great, a catcher has to be durable.

Told about the Bruce Lee comparison, Molina grinned Monday and said he did borrow from Alomar and take from Santiago. He had two brothers who caught in the majors and he adapted their habits as well. The late Dave Ricketts, a longtime coach for Molina, continues to influence Molina's positioning and how he does drills at the position to stay sharp. He said another person would "be a surprise," because Jose Oquendo, the Cardinals' infield coach, has "taught me more about catching that maybe you'd believe."

Molina has put pieces from all these mentors and coaches and friends and family together into a style of catching that is entirely his own. That is a part of his shares.

HIS MOTIVATION. THE BOTTOM LINE.

Walking out of Monday's media session, Molina stopped when the list got to that point. He put his hand on a reporter's shoulder and mentioned the young Puerto Ricans have it, too.

They consider more than legacy.

"Do you know why we play?" he asked. "We play to support that family. Dad. Mom. Uncles. Cousin. Home. This is our job. People behind us depend on us for what we do here, what we can provide for them. That's why we take it seriously. We're going to get better and better at whatever we do here so there you can help the people back home." ■

The Cardinals' Yadier Molina has caught in 1,778 games, a record for one major-league team.

Yadier Molina devoted his time last offseason to helping Puerto Rico recover from a hurricane.

IN HIS HERO'S FOOTSTEPS

Veteran catcher is fifth Cardinal to be honored as humanitarian

By Derrick Goold
October 25, 2018

The young, rising players from Puerto Rico have a nickname they use at times for Cardinals catcher Yadier Molina, and it has a spread through the national team to headlines and social media, and on Wednesday night at the World Series Boston manager Alex Cora mentioned it.

El Lider.

"I call him the leader because he's the leader of our national team. He's the leader of the St. Louis Cardinals. And he's the leader on the field," Cora said. "But off the field, he became the leader last year."

Less than 48 hours after the Cardinals' season ended a year ago, Molina, with thousands of dollars in supplies in tow, jetted to Puerto Rico to aid his home island in its recovery from the destructive force of Hurricane Maria. The days were long, the needs great and the destruction more profound than he expected. Molina would later describe it as "a nightmare down there."

As he cleared roads, repaired roofs and delivered food and water to neighborhoods near where he grew up, Molina was driven by a devotion to home and a lesson from his family — the same traits Major League Baseball mentioned Wednesday as it presented him its highest humanitarian honor.

Molina received this year's Roberto Clemente Award, the commissioner's office announced before Game 2 of the World Series. The award, named for the Hall of Fame outfielder who died on a relief mission on New Year's Eve 1972, goes annually to a player who captures the spirit of Clemente, on and off the field, through "extraordinary character, community involvement, (and) philanthropy." Molina's wife, Wanda, who helped him establish Foundation 4 (Fundacion 4), attended the presentation at Fenway Park, representing Yadier. He remained with Puerto Rico's national under-23 team at a world tournament in Colombia.

"He was like our legend — what he did, what he died for," Molina said in a phone interview from Colombia. "We have to share everything that he was, (that) he did when he was alive, on the field and off the field. … Roberto Clemente, he was one of my heroes back in the day — still one of my heroes — and just to have this award means a lot to me and to my family. For the people in Puerto Rico, we've been through many (challenges). We didn't do it thinking of this award, but just receiving this award makes us proud, makes us proud."

Molina is the fifth Cardinal to win the award — more than any other organization — and he joins former teammate Carlos Beltran and Carlos Delgado to become the third Puerto Rico-born player to win the award named for Puerto Rico's cherished son, Clemente. A fourth winner, Edgar Martinez, grew up in Puerto Rico after being born in New York. Each organization nominates a candidate for the Clemente, and a blue-ribbon committee's vote is mixed with a fan vote and the Clemente family's choice to determine the winner. Molina won the fan vote by one of the largest margins in the award's history, an official said.

He was also the top choice of Roberto's widow, Vera Clemente.

"One of the closest things to Roberto's heart was his beloved island of Puerto Rico," Vera said at Wednesday's presentation. "And Yadi's commitment to help the Puerto Rican community heal after such a catastrophic event embodies Roberto's philanthropic spirit. It is my honor to welcome Yadi to this wonderful family of Roberto Clemente Award winners."

In the days after Hurricane Maria pulverized the island in late September 2017 and left most of it without power, Molina and his wife began planning how best to help. He began raising money and collecting supplies while the team that helps run his foundation figured out how to secure a plane to deliver the goods. The donations and purchases filled seven industrial-sized crates, and Molina led the distribution throughout the Vega Alta neighborhoods he roamed as a boy. During his call with reporters from Colombia, Molina described how the days started at 6 a.m. and lasted until 1 a.m.

Cora told a story Wednesday about Molina visiting Utuado, where Houston outfielder George Springer's mother is from, and how the Cardinals catcher went door to door delivering bags of ice and food. The literature given Clemente voters details how in the same area Molina met an elderly diabetic man who needed insulin but was unable to move because of a leg amputation. Molina arranged transportation for him to a medical facility, "saving his life."

Molina said the sensation he had after 14 days there was like "drowning."

"As soon as we landed in Puerto Rico we saw all the destruction of the houses, the mountains, it was crazy," Molina said. "There were no mountains. No trees there. And the people — no power. They need too much help. I was like in shock."

Molina has raised more than $800,000 for relief efforts, and he said that he intends to launch other relief efforts and fundraisers through social media. Through his and his wife's foundation, they have also raised money for a safe house for battered children, to purchase anesthesia equipment for Puerto Rico's

Children's Hospital and its pediatric oncology ward, and to deliver Thanksgiving turkeys to families in his home neighborhood, Barrio Kuilan.

Beltran listed many of those acts as he celebrated Molina's Clemente candidacy Wednesday, adding in a text: "As a winner of the Roberto Clemente Award, I'm very proud of him. I personally know how much Roberto Clemente and Puerto Rico mean to Yadier. There is much more that he does in the island that he doesn't want people to know about. In the end, he is using his time and platform as an athlete not only to impact the team that he plays for but also to impact the community!"

As he prepared to manage Puerto Rico's national team Tuesday, Molina described how omnipresent Clemente was in his youth. His mother had a picture of Clemente in their home. At school, he and other students had to do reports on Clemente, his career

and his death in a plane crash on the way to help earthquake survivors in Nicaragua.

Molina's father, Benjamin Sr., was highly decorated as a baseball player in Puerto Rico and statues of him and his three sons, all of whom played catcher in the majors, stand at a stadium near their hometown. A decade ago, Benjamin Sr. had a heart attack near home plate at a field he had just raked for a youth team. Molina said this week that his father didn't play on the same team with Clemente, but did share a field with him once for practice.

And later, Benjamin Sr. shared a lesson.

"Hey, you know Roberto Clemente is a good player, right?" his father asked.

"I was like, 'Yeah, he's one of the greatest,'" Yadier recalled. "'He was even better outside the lines.' Those words I keep in my mind, and that's why this award means a lot to me." ∎

Sitting in front of a mattress and other items from a home damaged by Hurricane Maria, Cardinals catcher Yadier Molina meets with residents near his hometown of Vega Alta, Puerto Rico in 2017.

2020 - 2022

St. Louis Cardinals Albert Pujols talks with Yadier Molina during a pitching change in the sixth inning after hitting a single to score Tyler O'Neill against the Arizona Diamondbacks at Busch Stadium on Sunday, May 1, 2022.

Franchise cornerstones Wainwright and Molina enter final year of their contracts as team prepares for 60-game dash.

GREATS 'FOREVER LINKED'

Winning combo of Molina, Wainwright race time for another title with Cards

By Derrick Goold
July 19, 2020

The Cardinals' way from the players' parking lot into Busch Stadium passes through a hall where Yadier Molina and Adam Wainwright's names join lists of award-winners, and then leads to the clubhouse where their numbers could soon hang, alongside other icons. The moment a player walks inside is when the fables told about this winning pair reach a similar lesson: One or both arrived earlier, already waiting, already working.

Former Cardinal Matt Adams got up early one Sunday thinking this time, for sure, he would finally beat Molina to the ballpark for a day game the veteran had off. "Nope," Adams confessed. "Pull in, go to park — beside Yadi's car." Michael Wacha ducked into the video room to get an early jump scouting an upcoming series only to find the two teammates who set the example beat him to the computers, still setting the example. Annually, young catchers arrive to spring workouts at dawn and learn Molina even beats the sun to practice. As longtime friend Skip Schumaker described, "You don't have to tell Yadi to be in the cage at 5 o'clock in the morning for blocking balls with (late coach) Dave Ricketts. He's already there waiting for Dave Ricketts."

The stories weave from the clocks they set to the standards they do. This past season, as frustration seethed that their record was less than their talent, the Cardinals called a players-only meeting. Reliever Andrew Miller described how they gathered and gravitated, instinctively, into a "pileup" around Molina's locker. Where else to go for direction? It's a rite of summer for a young pitcher to get a tip from Wainwright. He's shared spiritual support for countless teammates, once rented a car for a reliever he saw walking to work, and this summer offered Korean lefty Kwang Hyun Kim some semblance of home while Kim was quarantined away from his family. A year ago, as Jack Flaherty mourned the sudden death of a dear friend, a knock came at his hotel room door. Wainwright was there for him.

That's what all the stories share. Molina and Wainwright are always there, ever present.

They have been as much a constant for the club as championship expectations. As living history, they've been a part of the team longer than the current ballpark and soaked up more champagne than the clubhouse carpet. With one on the mound and the other behind the plate, they are St. Louis baseball's most emblematic and beloved pair of Cardinals perched at a distance since Branch Rickey put two birds on a bat.

"Their love of competition, their commitment, their trust in each other, their intelligence and then their championships — that's a bond as tight as any you can possibly have," said Hall of Famer Tony La Russa, the winningest manager in Cardinals history. "It would be real special if they had normal careers for this long. Being champions makes them classic. They are in the conversation with the group of the greatest Cardinals. The real mentors, like they are, they'll talk about those guys forever."

Forged in October, a partnership continues the autumn of its tenure with a season unlike any before. Due to a global pandemic that stopped the 2020 season before it started, the Cardinals will open their 129th year in the National League on July 24th at Busch against Pittsburgh. From there, a 60-game mad dash for the playoffs. For the defending National League Central champs and reigning NL Manager of the Year Mike Shildt, it's a short burst to assert a self-improved offense, anchored by Paul Goldschmidt and outfitted with slugging shortstop Paul DeJong and bounce-back candidate Matt Carpenter. For Jack Flaherty, it's a chance to show his historic second half was a teaser and he's ready to ascend to ace.

For Wainwright, at 38, it's three months to decide if he'll pitch another year. For Molina, at 38, it's one more chance to become the first Cardinal ever to appear in five World Series.

For an organization, it's an inflection point.

The return to the postseason in 2019 started the bridge from one of the most successful eras in Cardinals history to what comes next. A new clutch of core Cardinals is revealing itself, and must. For the first time in their long career together Wainwright and Molina, the nucleus of the modern Cardinals, will both be free agents this fall. Their 16th season together is the longest for a duo in Cardinals history, surpassing Stan Musial and Red Schoendienst, and ties Atlanta's John Smoltz and Chipper Jones in recent NL history. Their next start as a battery will be No. 279, playoffs included. With six starts together, Molina and Wainwright have more than any pitcher-catcher combo since baseball's expansion in the 1960s.

Wainwright debuted on Sept. 11, 2005, and with Molina has seen the Cardinals win 1,246 games. They have one losing season together. Only the Dodgers, Yankees, and Red Sox have more wins than the Cardinals in the Molina-Wainwright Era. They have nine postseason berths, trailing only the Yankees and Dodgers, and yet have more World Series titles (two) and pennants (three). No active players have been teammates longer. Few tandems can claim as much shared success. They've been there, done that, had to wring the celebratory suds out of the T-shirt. And yet, there is a truer way to measure how they've enriched the Cardinals' tradition.

How it looks when they're no longer there.

"It's going to happen someday, and it's going to be weird," former Cardinals ace Chris Carpenter said. "It's the stamp you put on new guys and what they pass on that makes a solid, lasting organization. Does

Yadi have a certain stamp? Does Waino have a certain stamp? Absolutely. I brought that up to (the team) this spring — what do you want this ballclub to look like 10 years from now? When everyone, 40 years from now, is talking about the Jack Flaherty and Paul DeJong Era, what do you want them to say? The Mike Shildt Era — what do you want that to be? Everybody is going to go sometime. People are going to leave. Players aren't going to be here.

"Think of the names that are here — Yadi, Waino — and the stamps they've left for you. What is that legacy you're going to leave behind?"

'WE'VE GROWN UP TOGETHER'

When these two birds of a feather first met they were even closer than they have been at their best, but their intentions couldn't have been farther apart.

On May 9, 2003, the Greenville Braves visited the Cardinals' Class AA affiliate for a game celebrated because of that night's Tennessee Smokies starter, phenom Rick Ankiel, on his return to the majors. Dan Haren started the night before — part of the right-left showcase of the Cardinals' future. After Ankiel's two innings, the game came unwound. Schumaker was thrown out at home to force extra innings. Hours before being promoted to Class AAA Memphis John Gall punctuated a seven-run comeback with a walk-off homer in the 13th. Somewhere in that overstuffed box score the Smokies catcher faced the Braves' starter and singled.

Mr. Wainwright, meet Mr. Molina.

Twenty-one years to the day after Willie McGee was promoted to St. Louis and joined Ozzie Smith, the Cardinals' latest dynamic duo shared a field for the first time — as opponents. Later in 2003, the Cardinals acquired Wainwright in a franchise-redefining trade. A battery was born. During the next decade, Molina caught Wainwright's Triple-A debut (2004), his first major-league start (2007), his first postseason start (2009), and his first World Series start (2013). When Molina became the 10th Cardinal — and first since 1946 — to play in a fourth World Series, the pitch that made it official came from Wainwright.

"We've grown up together," Wainwright said. "We turned from little kids to men to dads together. We're family."

"We're brothers," Molina said. "When I grow up I want to be like him."

Their early dinner conversations centered on what happens in the 60 feet, 6 inches between them. Over time, baseball closed that gap. Similarities bloomed. A kid from an island off the coast of Georgia and a kid from an island in the Caribbean were both schooled in the game by older brothers. They're both pranksters. Molina turned to Wainwright for advice on starting a charity. Wainwright leaned on Molina to "shoot me straight" as he attempted a return from injuries.

As their friendship galvanized, their careers bronzed. Molina won the first of his nine Gold Glove Awards in 2008. In 2009, Wainwright started his run of four top-three finishes for the Cy Young Award in six years. Elbow surgery sidelined Wainwright during the 2011 World Series, but in the months that followed, as Albert Pujols left and Carpenter fought injury, what teammates saw happening naturally did officially: It was Molina's and Wainwright's team.

"A lot of winning has surrounded those two guys," Cubs manager David Ross said. Added Reds first baseman Joey Votto: "I think they would both agree their relationship together and the connection they have was built through challenging, high-stress situations. They have been a very successful battery."

"That battery mate is as good as anybody in the game in terms of going out there and competing, and laying it all on the line," said St. Louis native and World Series champ Max Scherzer, Washington's ace. "And they've done it year in, year out, they've won World Series titles together. From watching them from afar, I have the utmost respect of how they go out and play the game, and how they compete."

At that highest-stress moment, during a chilly October night in Queens, their wives, Wanda Molina and Jenny Wainwright, were back in St. Louis watching Game 7 of the 2006 NLCS. With a newborn, Jenny didn't travel. Wanda kept her company. Their families were growing and growing together. They shared the same couch, the same nerves, the same cheer as Molina homered, and the same apprehension. Adam joked, "They were biting on each other's fingernails." With the bases loaded, the Mets' Carlos Beltran up, and a pennant fluttering in the balance, Wainwright watched from the mound for a sign. The wives peered in, too. Molina shook off his plan to throw a fastball and urged the rookie pitcher to trust him.

"For crying out loud, in the biggest moment of my career, he calls a first-pitch changeup to the best hitter in the world at the time," Wainwright said. "Because he had a feeling? I had to completely trust him. And I always have since. Being around him — how do I say this? — I just feel calm."

The changeup set up the curve that clinched the pennant, and by the end of the month a slider claimed the World Series title. Strikeouts, both times. Molina gave Wainwright the baseball from the curve. The catcher kept the slider as a prized souvenir.

Like the best Cardinals twosomes, they knew how to make a first impression. Musial and Schoendienst's first season together was 1946, a championship year. Bob Gibson and Lou Brock had their first full Cardinals season together on the way to the 1964 title. Smith and McGee debuted as Cardinals in 1982, and they both scored a run in the World Series Game 7 win. At the end of their first full season together, Wainwright and Molina leaped into each other's arms.

"I've got a bunch of memories, but my favorites are every time we jump into a hug," Molina said. "You talk about the Cardinal Way, you talk about the names that mean everything to this franchise, and you need to add one: Waino. He is out there to win. We share that mindset. But you can't win championships every year. You can win a lot of good people that you know. You can win a lot of friendships. And I've been lucky enough to do that."

THEY'LL ALWAYS BE A 'TANDEM'

With his family beside him in the car, Wainwright considered the question this past week from a reporter before repeating it.

"How much do we think about what it means being together?"

He had a story.

In the clubhouse this month, Wainwright and Molina — who he usually calls by his full name, "Yadier" — reunited and talked about a common reality. Molina is coming to the end of a three-year extension, and Wainwright is on a one-year contract. Molina wants to play two more years, preferably with the Cardinals. If he plays, Wainwright wants to be with the Cardinals. The unknown is the Cardinals. The truncated 2020 season and its reduced revenue will influence the 2021 payroll. Uncertainty abounds.

"Neither of us wants to go anywhere. That's true. We say it. We mean it," Wainwright said. "What if the Cardinals say they want to move on from both of us? If that happens, we'd have to think about going somewhere else. You ask how much we think about being together. He says, 'Let's go somewhere together.' That's how much."

Molina says Wainwright has shown what it means to "be mentally strong and the best kind of teammate." Wainwright says he hopes the next generation "looks at all the winning that happened and how we did it together. There's proof it worked."

When a teammate eventually does walk into the clubhouse to find neither Wainwright nor Molina there, they may be gone but they're not going anywhere. They're as permanent as the titles they've won. A pitcher not yet drafted will receive the same advice Wainwright gave Flaherty. A catcher not yet signed will hear how Molina ate wild pitches for breakfast. They're in the hall, on the wall, and in the fabric of the Cardinals.

They don't have to be here to be a presence.

"I think about a team without them, I do," coach Stubby Clapp said. "And then I think we'll always see them outside the ballpark, together, as a tandem statue." ∎

Adam Wainwright and Yadier Molina celebrate after winning Game 5 and the World Series in 2006 vs. Detroit at Busch Stadium.

MOLINA MILESTONE IN WIN

Catcher makes it to 2,000 hits as Redbirds record a key victory

By Derrick Goold
September 25, 2020

During Thursday night's game at a cardboard fan-infused Busch Stadium, the silence of the absent crowd for a game with playoff implications was the sound manager Mike Shildt and first baseman Paul Goldschmidt noticed as they spoke near the dugout steps. Imagine the hum of the place, they said, with the Brewers in town, a postseason berth on the line, and there, at the tip of Yadier Molina's bat, to electrify the evening a spark of history.

For the first time, a Cardinals player would reach 2,000 hits and zero fans would be in the stands to see it.

His teammates had to rise to the occasion.

Molina's second single of the Cardinals' tone-setting 4-2 victory against the Brewers on Thursday landed in center field for the 2,000th of his career.

He joined friend and former teammate Albert Pujols and four Hall of Famers as the only six players with 2,000 hits for the Cardinals, and the noise that could not come from fans in the ballpark came instead from a standing ovation in the dugout, echoing out to the applause from the bullpen. For a second, social distancing and masks took a break for celebration.

"You just got a chance to have a baseball moment," Shildt said. "Probably one of the biggest games where we missed not having a crowd, because you know what the crowd would have been like this weekend, and missed having it for Yadi. So we gave him a standing ovation. It was just a fun moment. A moment to pause and honor a great accomplishment for a great player."

During a lopsided game in Kansas City this past week, Shildt gave Molina the option of coming out of the game, resting his legs, his knees, his thrice-bruised hand for this four-day, five-game decisive series against the Brewers. Molina declined because he wanted one more at-bat. He wanted one more at-bat because he wanted a hit.

His clock was running.

Molina, a free agent at season's end without the guarantee of a return to the only team he's known, had 2,000 in sight, and wanted to reach with birds on his bat.

"It was on my mind," he said late Thursday. "My mind is always about the team and winning. I won't lie to you. It was on my mind to get that this year, wearing this uniform because you never know what's going to happen."

Molina's single gave ceremony to a game already rich with substance.

The win gave the Cardinals (28-26) a two-game lead on the chasing Brewers (27-29) and gained a game on the first-place Cubs (32-25). With four scheduled games remaining — including Friday's doubleheader at Busch Stadium — the Cardinals are simultaneously chasing a division title and a fifth seed into the postseason. They have a half-game edge on

Cincinnati for the second-place finish in the division and automatic playoff berth that goes with it.

Opportunity after opportunity to pull away from the Brewers on the scoreboard and in the standings rolled by inning after inning Thursday night, and it took a rookie delivering a lead as prelude to the veteran adding the dash of history.

Dylan Carlson hit a two-run homer to snap a 1-1 tie in the fourth inning, and he added an RBI double late in the game to widen the lead. Each of Carlson's hits came after Dexter Fowler had fallen behind 0-2 in the count and come back to work a walk. Fowler's fourth-inning walk off Brewers starter Corbin Burnes sent obvious concern through the Milwaukee dugout. Brewers manager Craig Counsell marched onto the mound on the heels of a trainer trotting in the same direction. Counsell appeared to make a gesture to the bullpen for a righthander, and there was an urgency to the visit that implied Burnes, a league-leader with his 1.77 ERA, had a physical ailment. Yet, he remained in the game.

"Same approach," Carlson said of watching the events. "Ready to rock."

He did on a cutter, and a batter later Burnes was lifted with lower-back discomfort that he has experienced in other recent starts.

Carlson did with Fowler on first base what so many of the other Cardinals struggled to do with runners in scoring position. The Cardinals went one-for-16 with runners in scoring position, and the speed bump to bigger innings came in the middle of the order where slumps abound. Cleanup hitter Matt Carpenter brought a two-for-30 into Thursday's game. Brad Miller, the longtime cleanup hitter until recently, takes a three-for-25 into the weekend. Paul DeJong snapped a zero-for-18 with a double in the seventh.

"Goldy got the guy in, Dylan brought in three, and it was enough," Shildt said. "Always want more. The nice part would be to have that finishing blow to make it a five-, six-, seven-run game."

Before Andrew Miller came into the secure the win with a save and the tying run on base for former MVP

Christian Yelich, the game hinged around a moment in the fifth with starter Kwang Hyun Kim. The rookie, who joined the Cardinals from the KBO, had needed 27 pitches to get through the fourth, and the Brewers were stressing his pitch count again. He walked the Brewers' top two hitters, including Yelich, to bring former MVP Ryan Braun, a righthanded hitter, to the plate. The Cardinals had reliever Giovanny Gallegos warmed and ready for the moment, but Shildt stuck with Kim.

Kim got a fly out and assured a fifth inning to finish his rookie season unbeaten, at 3-0. Shildt said he leaned on the usual adviser when it came to sticking with Kim.

"Yadi is like the quarterback of the team," he said. "You trust the quarterback."

In addition to Pujols, the players who had 2,000 hits with the Cardinals are Lou Brock, Stan Musial, Rogers Hornsby, and Enos Slaughter. Molina is the 10th player in history to play two-thirds of his games at catcher and reach 2,000 hits. Seven of the nine catchers with more hits, including Ted Simmons and Yogi Berra, have been elected to Cooperstown. When his 2,000th hit landed in center field, it was Molina's older brother, Bengie, who had the call on the Cardinals' Spanish-radio network.

That thought brought a grin to the catcher who a manager once said didn't have to get another hit to start every game for him.

"When I came up I was focused on my defense," said Molina, a nine-time Gold Glove-award winner. "A lot of people in the media they just give up on me and my offense. Obviously I was a poor hitter. But I worked hard to prove them wrong. Right now I'm in this moment and thank you to them for giving me the motivation. … It's been many years. You want to get to this point. I'm finally here.

I'll enjoy it." ■

Yadier Molina follows through in the seventh inning Thursday as he connects for his 2,000th hit, his second hit of the night.

HOW DID MOLINA STEAL THAT STRIKEOUT? 'HE IS A WIZARD,' SAYS WAINWRIGHT

By Derrick Goold
October 2, 2020

SAN DIEGO — What Yadier Molina expected to be a curveball, down and away and out of reach of Fernando Tatis Jr., instead was a fastball up and in and became a magic trick.

In the third inning Thursday night at Petco Park, Adam Wainwright took the sign for a 2-2 pitch to the San Diego Padres' No. 2 hitter. He and catcher Molina got their signals crossed, and with Molina expecting a curveball, Wainwright delivered a fastball. What happened next neither of them or Tatis could believe. Wainwright's fastball clipped off the handle of Tatis' bat, and Molina's mitt swallowed it for a foul-tip strikeout.

"He is a wizard," Wainwright said.

The out was significant at the time, innings before Tatis unloaded two home runs and powered the Padres to an 11-9 victory, because it came with two runners on base and gave Wainwright an escape hatch to the third inning, his final full inning. Wainwright had three strikeouts in his Game 2 start, and this one left Tatis shaking his head and the Cardinals' veteran starting grinning on the mound. Molina, in his 100th playoff game, shrugged.

He's pulled this sleight of hand before, and not always with his hand.

"I don't know if it was my fault or his fault but he was crossed up on that," Wainwright explained after the game "He was looking for a breaking ball down and away at 75 mph, and I threw 102-fastball up and in. I don't know how he caught it. Obviously it wasn't 102. It was hard enough for it not to be a curveball. Nobody else catches that.

"Amazing. Truly amazing."

The Padres' have seen such sorcery before from Molina, and it happened with one of Tatis' current teammates. On June 12, 2018, Miles Mikolas delivered a pitch that Padres first baseman Eric Hosmer fouled back. The two-strike pitch clipped Molina's glove, and then wedged at his hip, where the leg meets the torso in Molina's squat. By rule, that is a foul-tip catch even though Molina did not keep the ball in his mitt. Andy Green, the Padres' manager at the time, came out to argue the call, and home plate umpire Chris Segal explained the reason for his call: The ball hit Molina's mitt first. That's key.

The rule governing foul-tip strikeouts insists that the difference between a foul tip and a pop up or foul ball is that the foul-tip strikeout is "sharp and direct" to the catcher's mitt. And then also legally caught.

That means a two-strike pitch fouled back into a catcher's mask and stuck there is not a foul-tip strikeout. Neither is a two-strike pitch that is fouled back and caught in the catcher's chest protector. Unless … unless … either of those foul tips nick the mitt on the way. That's what happened with Hosmer back in June 2018. His foul tip went off Molina glove and then was trapped at Molina's waist for a legal catch. And that wasn't even the first time that Molina did that.

At Wrigley Field, on July 11, 2013, Randy Choate delivered a pitch to Nate Schierholtz. The Cubs' outfielder took a mighty swing, caught a piece of the baseball, and sent it back toward Molina. The foul ball caromed down off the bat, caught the lower edge of Molina's mitt, and then got trapped in the crease between Molina's right leg and his torso. True to the rule, because the ball did not miss the mitt entirely, he umpire called Schierholtz out on the foul-tip strikeout.

The snag of Tatis' foul tip was sharper, more direct. But no less remarkable.

"Pretty amazing, really," manager Mike Shildt called it.

Wainwright said he delivered the "102-mph fastball" in part because he's thrown so much to Molina — this was their 14th start in the postseason together — that he knows the catcher's habit. Molina will sometimes misdirect the hitter by lining up outside, on the far edge of the plate as if to catch a curveball away and then bounce back to catch the fastball inside. That's what Wainwright believed he was doing, not suspecting at all that they had their signs awry.

The fastball he threw came in at 89 mph.

Molina snapped his mitt in direction of the up-and-in pitch.

Tatis turned and then had no interest in offering at the pitch, but his at drooped just enough behind him that the pitch ricocheted off it. Tatis had no interest in swinging at the pitch, and yet his lean toward it had put the bat in its path. On the way to reaching for where he thought the pitch was going, Molina's mitt encountered the pitch where it had been redirected. He held on, and Tatis was out.

"As we walked off the field," Wainwright said, "I asked him, 'How did you catch that?'"

Wainwright recalled Molina's reply.

"I have no idea." ∎

Yadier Molina catches Eric Hosmer's foul ball during the eighth inning of Game 2 of the National League Wild-Card Series.

SIGNING RESTORES SOME NORMALCY TO A CRAZY TIME

By Jeff Gordon
February 10, 2021

Like everyone else, the Cardinals want to get their old life back in 2021.

So the *team* just had to pull iconic catcher Yadier Molina back from the free-agent pool. It took months, but president of baseball operations John Mozeliak finally did.

"The community, the franchise, the teammates, all the coaching staff . . . they wanted me back," Molina said during his video call with reporters. "I wanted to be back here.

"In my mind, it was St. Louis (as) my first choice."

Any other outcome would been unsettling, even in the midst of all the other COVID-19 chaos in sports.

The thought of Molina playing in any other uniform is absurd. The sight of him decked out in New York Yankees pinstripes or wearing the Los Angeles Angels halo logo would have been cringeworthy.

After 17 seasons, 2,025 regular season games, 101 postseason games, nine All-Star Game invitations and nine Gold Gloves in the STL, how could he possibly play anywhere else?

He must finish his career as a Cardinal, earn his plaque in the Baseball Hall of Fame, get his statue outside Busch Stadium and take his place with Stan Musial, Lou Brock, Bob Gibson, Ozzie Smith as franchise lifers.

Any other outcome would leave fans disoriented. Molina has been the constant they have relied upon while so many other players came and went.

But they should not take his public service for granted. Molina's pride is immense.

That pride pushed him to overcome his early struggles at the plate, just as Ozzie did. It drove him to remake his body and extend his career through an intense conditioning regime.

That pride prompted social media hubris that occasionally rubbed folks the wrong way. It also prevented him from accepting a contract that he deemed insulting.

So he played out his free agency. He was hoping to get a two-year contract to respect his work — and, given his success, why wouldn't he?

Molina can't see himself slowing down. He's willed himself this far. If a harder push is needed then, he will just push harder.

While most veterans were resting their bodies this winter, Molina played in the Puerto Rico League for his brother Jose before competing in the Caribbean Series too.

Ultimately the contract issue worked itself out. He settled for one year and $9 million, plus another potential $1 million in bonus money. That seems reasonable after his previous three-year, $60 million contract.

"When you're in free agency, anything can happen," Molina said. "You get teams calling you. It's a process you don't want to experience, and at the same time you want to experience it. It was a slow process. I never had the doubt. I knew this day would come. I was expecting sooner, but it is what it is."

So Molina and cohort Adam Wainwright are back for another run. With the addition of Nolan Arenado, the Cardinals should extend their string of 13 consecutive winning seasons.

"I love Waino," Molina said. "He's my brother. Then you add Arenado there, why not come back? We feel good about this team. Hopefully we stay healthy and get the job done."

Reaching the postseason for the eighth time in 11 seasons is an achievable goal. This team is still built on pitching and defense and Molina bolsters both.

So this signing is not just a marketing move, although Molina can still move some product. That's no small matter with the franchise trying to recoup nine-digit revenue losses.

Both Molina and Wainwright were instrumental in the team's push through coronavirus adversity and into the playoff bracket last season.

They have helped maintain the franchise's winning culture year after year after year. They have led through words, example and performance.

Wainwright, who turns 40 this season, was 5-3 with a 3.15 earned run average in 10 starts last year. He can still fill a key role in the rotation.

Molina, who turns 39, remains an excellent catcher. Teams still don't run on him. Pitchers still listen to him. So do umpires.

He remains a presence behind the plate, playing with an edge. He remains a presence in the clubhouse, especially with the hurlers.

Adam Wainwright jokes with catcher Yadier Molina after they completed a bullpen session during St. Louis Cardinals spring training on Thursday, Feb. 13, 2020, in Jupiter, Fla.

"For me, you have to be there every day for them," Molina said. "That's No. 1. You have to care. For me, I care for the pitchers."

And Molina can still hit. He batted .317 with runners on base last season and .364 with runners in scoring position and two outs.

He adapts his swing to the pitcher, the ball-and-strikes count and the game situation. Just about every other hitter in Our National Pastime is trying to yank fly balls with an elevated launch angle over extreme fielding shifts.

He and Wainwright enjoy sharing their wisdom. They will help mentor all those live-armed pitchers the franchise is pinning future hopes upon.

Molina can also help develop back-up Andrew Knizner and young Ivan Herrera, the organization's Next New Thing at the position. Their progress (or lack thereof) will add to speculation about who will catch in 2022.

In the meantime, there is a NL Central title to compete for in '21. Molina will restore a sense of baseball normalcy while leading that charge. ■

MOLINA SET TO CATCH 2,000TH GAME

By Derrick Goold
April 14, 2021

That first at-bat would come in the second inning, the cherished first hit would come three innings after that, and a runner would dare to try and steal in the eighth; he was unsuccessful. But a career about to reach a singular milestone truly began that summer night in Pittsburgh when Woody Williams uncoiled from his windup and delivered a pitch.

Awaiting it, in a crouch that will one day be bronzed, was Yadier Molina.

"It is so long ago, not only for a catcher — but 17 years since I threw him that first pitch and so long ago that I don't even feel like baseball was part of my life anymore," Williams said Tuesday from Texas. "And to see that he's still doing it and still doing it at a high level. If I'm one of those pitchers on that staff, especially one who has struggled in recent years, I'm a bobblehead.

"My head is just going up and down on the mound," Williams added. "He puts down a sign, and I'm throwing that pitch."

What began June 3, 2004, at PNC Park with six shutout innings from Williams and a win for those runaway Redbirds will continue Wednesday afternoon at Busch Stadium with what's scheduled to be Molina's 2,000th game behind the plate. Only the sixth catcher in major-league history to receive 2,000 games, Molina will be the first to do so entirely with one team.

Molina received Tuesday night off after manager Mike Shildt canvassed his regulars and offered Molina either that night or Wednesday's day game as a break. Andrew Knizner's start at catcher Tuesday sets up Yadi2K with longtime teammate and "brother" Adam Wainwright delivering the pitches. Wainwright recently marveled at how Molina, 38, has revved into the season with 12 hits through the first 10 games and a .998 OPS.

"I mean — staying immortal like he always is?" Wainwright said. "Nothing he does surprises me. He's a little heavier than he was last year, got a little more pop in the bat. You can tell he's feeling good, moving well."

It is possible to measure Molina's career in statistics. He's one of three active players with at least 2,000 hits, and earlier this season he passed Hall of Famer Johnny Bench for eighth all-time among catchers with his 382nd double. Molina will have caught 76.6% of the 2,609 games the Cardinals have played since his debut, not including his NL-record (for any position) 101 playoff games. He craves his 10th Gold Glove award and sets out to lead the league in innings behind the plate. Since 2004, Molina's 25.4 defense Wins Above Replacement are second only to sublime shortstop Andrelton Simmons (25.8), according to Baseball-Reference.com. The next closest active catcher is Salvador Perez at 13.4 dWAR, and for context teammate Nolan Arenado, who debuted in 2013, has a 15.6 dWAR.

There have been eight Platinum Gloves awarded in the NL. Arenado has won the previous four; Molina won the first four.

Or, the longevity of Molina's career can be measured in events. He debuted 16 years, 10 months, and seven days ago. A fan born that day can drive to his 2,000th game today. His debut was years before Netflix started to stream (2007), Twitter started a feed (2006), or his personal favorite Instagram filtered in (2010). The iPhone was an idea. Pluto was still a planet. The Astros batted pitchers in the NL not battered trashcans in the AL. During Molina's time with the Cardinals, London won a bid to host the Olympic Games and hosted the Summer Games — almost nine years ago — and was about to host the Cardinals for two games before a pandemic limited travel.

"The way I put records like that into context and I do that like with Cal (Ripken Jr.) is you start to put that in the context of how many years that is of playing," Shildt said. "In Cal's case it's every day. In Yadi's case it's most every day. I don't know which one is more impressive because they're both amazing feats. You put 2,000 games into the context of 162-game regular season, and you say, OK, if he caught every single game how many years would that be. And you go — whoa."

It would be 12⅓ seasons.

Whoa.

"I think he could go out there and catch 150 games right now," Williams said. "You knew early on there was something special with him. It starts with humility. You learn a lot about the makeup of a person. It's just going about doing my job and for, good gracious, 20 years now or something silly he's done his job. It's incredible."

KIM BACK, PONCE TO BULLPEN

Kwang Hyun Kim, sidelined since spring because back soreness interrupted his throwing program, will rejoin the rotation Saturday, and start that afternoon against

Yadier Molina stretches before his home debut against the Houston Astros on Friday, June 4, 2004, in St. Louis.

the Phillies. His return shifts Daniel Ponce de Leon to the bullpen as the long reliever for at least the short term. Ponce de Leon, who is out of options and must pass through waivers to go to the minors or taxi squad, was available as soon as Tuesday for an overtaxed bullpen.

John Gant will remain in the rotation for the foreseeable future, Shildt said. The righthander completed five innings and allowed three runs on six hits Monday.

OVIEDO OPTIONED, WHITLEY UP

To import a fresh arm and setting themselves up for the shift to a six-man rotation later this month, the Cardinals swapped righthander Johan Oviedo for reliever Kodi Whitley on Tuesday. Oviedo returned to the alternate site, where he will have to remain at least 10 days unless called upon to replace an injured pitcher. ■

MILESTONE FOR MOLINA IN SETBACK

His 2,000th game as Cards catcher is a Nats win

By Rick Hummel

April 15, 2021

The game that really wasn't Wednesday at Busch Stadium can be dispatched in a few paragraphs. The Washington Nationals applied a 6-0 whipping on the Cardinals, who did little offensively and not a whole lot defensively in the outfield.

Two doubles and two singles represented the offense. "(Joe) Ross was pinpoint," said manager Mike Shildt of the Washington starter. "You tip your hat."

Shildt thought home plate umpire Sean Barber might have missed some close ones. And during a ninth-inning visit to perform a double switch, Shildt said to Barber, "Look, man, I'm going to take out my frustration on you."

Lane Thomas, getting his second start in center field, missed a diving catch for the second time in two starts. He also let a single get through for an error.

Yadier Molina acknowledges fans Wednesday, when he became the first player to catch in 2,000 games for only one team.

And, leaping against the wall for Ryan Zimmerman's third-inning home run which bounced off the concrete atop the left-center-field wall, Thomas came nowhere near it.

A catchable ball dropped for a double in left between Austin Dean and backtracking shortstop Edmundo Sosa, which probably was Dean's ball although Thomas was not far from it either.

"Maybe it wasn't the best day for (Thomas)," said Shildt. "But we'll move on and he'll move on."

Shildt is having to fill gaps in the outfield with Gold Glover Tyler O'Neill and Gold Glove finalist Harrison Bader injured — Dylan Carlson had his first start off Wednesday — and Shildt said bench coach Oli Marmol mentioned to him, "Now, I understand why you are always pushing for a holistic lineup."

Shildt said, "Defense is a part of the lineup. We need to play good, clean baseball. Not perfect. The game's hard. All we're asking for is make routine plays, be clean and be aggressive."

Shildt said he is giving players opportunities in the outfield and is hoping that those players will "take the experience and grow from it."

Or as starter Adam Wainwright, who likes the athleticism of the young outfielders, said, "If you're not the most comfortable out there, the ball will find you."

Basically, it was all downhill after ball one. That pitch was delivered by Wainwright and it merited a standing ovation as Wainwright stepped back off the mound and let his catcher, Yadier Molina, handling Wainwright for the 277th time, have the stage on the occasion of Molina becoming the first player to catch 2,000 games for one club.

It wound up that Wainwright would be leading those cheers.

"They came to me before the game and asked me, 'Do you mind if we take a brief pause after the first pitch, just for like 10 seconds?' Ten minutes, I don't care," said Wainwright.

The game was stopped as the fans, besides players and coaches, gave Molina a standing ovation. Molina saluted the fans and both clubs — the Cardinals were out front of the dugout and their bullpen was cheering too — and then was ready to return to action.

But Wainwright was not, standing well behind the mound and waving his arms wildly, imploring the fans for more. For all the times Molina has stood in front of home plate to honor properly (in his mind) a prominent former Cardinal when he came to bat, Wainwright was going to make Molina wait this time and try to make him laugh in the process (he did).

"I don't want to call him a clown. I don't laugh that often," said Molina.

"Pretty neat moment. I never expected that from Waino. He's one of the great human beings. He's been there for me for many years. I wish we could have a different result but that moment was a great moment."

Wainwright said, "How many times have I had a chance to do that in my career? Not one time in the regular season. And one time with Derek Jeter at the All-Star Game (in 2014 in Minneapolis)."

Wainwright led the applause for the retiring New York Yankees star on that night as Jeter led off and then laid a fastball over the plate, on which Jeter doubled.

"And today for Yadier Molina," said Wainwright. "Two of the greatest players of all time. It was a treat to be part of a moment like that. My regret is that we didn't win the game for him.

"Any time you hear 'only one in MLB history' to do anything, that's pretty cool," said Wainwright. "Catching 2,000 games, period, is kind of ridiculous anyways. And then, with the same team here in St. Louis the whole time ... he's a really special player in a really special place and I'm just glad we got to witness as much greatness as we have out of him over the years.

"I would have liked to have seen him take a Cal Ripken lap around the field."

Shildt said, "He definitely deserved the moment. That's an accomplishment I value very highly, for what that's worth. Think of all the different accomplishments that need to take place for that to have happened. You need to be a good player, for one. You need to be a consistent player. And you look at a guy who's hungry.

"Not that it's easy to be hungry during the games and during the season — that's when the fun part is. But it's the offseason dedication, it's the 6 o'clock in the morning coming to spring training. I'm out at the complex early in the morning and there's Yadi working.

"There's no coincidence that this guy's an unbelievable combination of skill sets. It was very special to be part of it with him."

Molina's Hall of Fame credentials are not an issue with Wainwright. "I already think he's first ballot. But, today just put a stamp on it," said Wainwright.

"Two thousand games. You don't get to catch 2,000 games anywhere, especially with one team, if you're just not an unbelievable player.

"Honestly he could have about 16 Gold Gloves (Molina has nine). Who's better than Yadier Molina behind the plate? If you ask the 29 other catchers in the game if they're better than Yadi behind the plate, there's not going to be a whole lot of guys who raise their hands and say, 'Yeah, I'm clearly better than Yadier Molina.' A once-in-a-lifetime catcher."

Molina singled in his first at-bat to extend his hitting streak to 10 games. But he flied out twice and fanned thereafter.

Molina told reporters that 2,000 "was just another number. I never go out there to make my numbers," he said. "If we would have won this game, it would have made it more special for me."

But Wainwright said, "I know that 2,000 was special for him. That just hard-seals a Hall of Fame career.

"We should have just postponed the game and made it Yadier Molina Day."

Molina said umpire Barber told him at one point, "That's a lot of games."

Replied Molina, "It happened fast." ∎

Cardinal catcher Yadier Molina bumps fists with first base coach Stubby Clapp on Wednesday, April 14, 2021, after extending his hitting streak to nine games in the first inning of a game against the Washington Nationals at Busch Stadium in St. Louis, Mo. The game marked Molina's 2000th start with the Cardinals.

St. Louis Cardinals catcher Yadier Molina (4) celebrates hitting a solo homer in the second inning during a game Cincinnati Reds and the St. Louis Cardinals in St. Louis on Friday, April 23, 2021.

'IT WILL BE MY FINAL SEASON'

Cardinals great Molina, contract in hand and red jacket waiting, says he'll retire after 2022

By Derrick Goold
August 26, 2021

He can already hear the reception he's going to get in 2022 as he takes his farewell tour of the National League Central, tugging on his mask and rising from the sunken dugout at Wrigley Field for his final start in front of the ivy or walking toward right field to meet a pitcher as they ready for a game in Cincinnati.

"All the boos," Yadier Molina said.

Ovations could follow.

Probably.

Maybe.

The Cardinals' catcher, one of the finest ever to play the position in NL history, talked for the first time Wednesday morning about his new contract for 2022 and confirmed that, yes, it will be his last season before he retires. The wish to play one more season prompted the time of negotiations with the Cardinals so that he could assure he'd finish his 19-year career with them.

"It will be my final season," Molina said during a Zoom conference with reporters. "It will be my final season. That's what I wanted to do. That's what my agent and myself came to (the Cardinals) and said, 'I want to stay here. I want to get it done this year.

"It's going to be my last year. I want to finish here in this great organization."

Family, friends, and other close associates have spent the past few years urging Molina to announce his retirement ahead of his final season so that he could get some of the ceremony, the celebration other All-Star players and franchise greats have received. In his press conference, he mentioned seeing the sendoffs that David Ortiz got in Boston and Yankees shortstop Derek Jeter received as he traveled around the majors in his final year, including a stop complete with gifts at Busch Stadium.

Molina's statement that he'll retire after the 2022 season also allows the Cardinals to plan ahead, perhaps even sketch up a logo.

Molina, who has caught more games for one team than any catcher in big-league history, approached the Cardinals a little more than a month ago about an extension. Conversations were scheduled for after the trade deadline, and they picked up momentum in the past week. The two sides agreed to a one-year, $10-million deal for 2022, and president of baseball operations called it both the oddest and swiftest negotiations that he can remember.

"When you watch them play a long and distinguished and Hall of Fame career with the organization, to have someone to want to stay and be a part of something from Day 1 to where their career ends is just remarkable in this day and age," Mozeliak said. "Anybody who was sitting on my side of table

realized here you have this treasure, this person who has been iconic for an organization, and what am I supposed to do — fight over money? Yadi knows us. We would try to do anything to resolve this."

Mozeliak and Molina both referred to each other as close friends throughout the press conference, and Molina referred to the "ups and downs, gives and takes" that close friends have through the years. Mozeliak oversaw the Cardinals' draft when Molina was selected in the fourth round, back in 2000. They have both risen in influence since.

"The man has earned a lot of respect," Mozeliak said.

When asked why now was the moment to decide on retiring, Molina smiled.

"It's enough," he said. "It's a long career."

Molina will turn 40 during his final season, and he'll be one of two catchers with 2,000 hits that had them all for the same team. Johnny Bench is the other. An All-Star this season, Molina will have a chance to earn an 11th All-Star invite and two seasons in which he could win a 10th Gold Glove Award. Only Bench and Ivan Rodriguez have more Gold Glove awards, and both are in the National Baseball Hall of Fame.

Molina said he will begin lobbying Adam Wainwright to return to the Cardinals so that battery will have a chance in 2022 to set the record for starts by a pitcher-catcher combo.

Molina grew up with the Cardinals, mentored by the late Dave Ricketts and around the greats such as Lou Brock and Bob Gibson and Red Schoendienst. Teams are no longer permitted to offer players personal service contracts as part of a playing contract, but the one-year extension does give Molina a bridge to go from playing for the Cardinals to spending his life around the Cardinals — visiting spring, working with young catchers, perhaps a larger presence at some point within the organization.

And, of course, a plaque awaits and somewhere the sketch of a statue exists.

"I can't wait to put that red jacket on," Molina said, grinning. ■

Cardinal catcher Yadier Molina celebrates at first base on Saturday Aug. 7, 2021, after a two-run RBI hit in the first inning of a game against the Kansas City Royals at Busch Stadium in St. Louis, Mo.

SET FOR NUMBER 300

Wainwright & Molina hit milestone as they near all-time record

By Derrick Goold
September 3, 2021

MILWAUKEE — As he drove alone in his rental car toward south Chicago and the resumption of a season once in doubt, Adam Wainwright found a place to pull over and stretch. Back spasms seized on him on the way to a start against the White Sox, the start that would bring the Cardinals back into their 2020 season from isolation, from a coronavirus quarantine they partially spent bunkered in the same Milwaukee hotel they call home this weekend.

The Cardinals had not played in more than two weeks and pitchers had been delivered baseballs by room service to do something, anything to invigorate their arms. Internally, there was deep consternation and deeper concern how to safely use pitchers and who could handle a cold start vs. the Sox. Wainwright raised his right hand.

On the side of the road, he loosened the knot in his back and considered the weight placed on his shoulder.

"I remember thinking, 'I'm about to set a tone for this entire season right now,'" Wainwright recalled. "This is really important."

He finished the drive to the ballpark as a familiar rush returned. Wainwright knew with certainty what no one else could.

This was a start an ace should make — and he would, again.

"That's a hard thing to fake," Wainwright said Wednesday, leaning against the bat rack in the visitors' dugout at Great American Ball Park. "Being a guy who was washed (up), who is completely done and then two years later being a guy where everyone is

St. Louis Cardinals catcher Yadier Molina (4) and starting pitcher Adam Wainwright (50) walk in from the bullpen after warm-ups before the start of a game between the Kansas City Royals and the St. Louis Cardinals at Busch Stadium in St. Louis on Friday, Aug. 6, 2021.

depending on you — that's a really fun moment for me. I knew last year that I needed to be on every time. I know this year I need to be on every time. And that takes me back to when I was the true No. 1. There was an idea that I'm effecting three, maybe four days for the rotation with what I'm about to do on this mound. It was important. It mattered. And everybody expected that from me and needed that from me. I loved that. I love that.

"Feeling needed like that really helps."

And it hasn't changed in the year since or year to come.

A week, which continued Thursday with the National League Pitcher of the Month honor for August, began with a personal milestone for Wainwright and will close with a professional — one that has become a driving force for his leaning toward a 2022 return.

Wainwright, who turned 40 on Monday, and catcher Yadier Molina will make their 300th career start together, as a battery, Friday night against the Brewers. It's the round number. And, there is a tone to set.

The Cardinals, grasping for a handle in the wild-card race, will play their next seven games against first-place teams and face a division-dominating Brewers team that won three consecutive this week to knock San Francisco out of the NL West lead.

After Molina-Wainwright, the next active tandem is Molina's 121 starts with Carlos Martinez. In the non-Molina division there's Boston's Christian Vazquez with pitcher Eduardo Rodriguez, at 104.

Molina and Wainwright are the fourth pair to reach that number together and the first since Detroit's Mickey Lolich and Bill Freehan did more than 46 years ago. Lolich and Freehan have the all-time lead with 324 starts together. The Cardinals' two birds of a feather can claim that record with health in 2022 — and Wainwright's return. Molina has already agreed to a one-year extension for 2022 and announced his plans to retire at the end of next season. He has started dropping hints to Wainwright, casually mentioning the history they could yet share or giving him non-verbal nudges.

Three or four times a game, Molina will make eye contact with Wainwright from across the dugout and raise his eyebrows just so.

"I know what he's thinking and he knows what I'm thinking," Wainwright said. "He hasn't put the full-court press on me yet."

Within the past two weeks, the Cardinals have approached Wainwright to discuss his plans for 2022. It was a brief talk, an opening volley. More discussions are forthcoming. The club intends to have a one-year offer waiting when their ace emeritus is ready, a club source described.

Adam Wainwright jokes with Yadier Molina after the two faced off in a live hitting session during spring training in 2009 in Jupiter, Fla.

Wainwright has steadfastly said conversations with family will shape his decision, and the Wainwrights have already begun those at home, he said. Wainwright's oldest daughter, born the same week he became the Cardinals' closer as a rookie in 2006, started high school. Raised with his brother by a single mother, Wainwright described how his youth is shaping his thinking because "I don't want to be the dad who missed everything. I had a dad who missed everything, and I don't want to be the dad that misses everything."

"If it was just a pitching decision, then it's a no-brainer for me," Wainwright continued. "I really love what I'm doing and enjoy competing and everything about pitching. I really enjoy pitching. If I was going to tell you today, I would say I'm probably going to pitch next year. Things change real quick in this world so I don't want to get too far ahead of myself. I don't want to be one of those athletes who retires three times.

"I want to know that I know that I know."

It was only three years ago it felt like the choice was made for him.

Before a start in San Diego in 2018, Wainwright felt two bones in his elbow clap together. His stomach ached. He felt ill. He knew. What he had to "trick them and mix and match and add and subtract and fight my way through" was also now going to hurt. Each pitch was preceded by a deep breath and a wish to throw one more. He made 79, walked six, and left the mound in the third inning for what he realized might be the last time. The pain on the backside of his right elbow was so severe it creeped into everything else he tried to do. He couldn't strum the opening chords of a song on his guitar.

"Not one note," he said. "There was no enjoyment factor at all in throwing a baseball, in throwing anything. There was no enjoyment in picking up a fork."

There was no thought of another start, let alone a 350th of his career or a 300th with Molina. Rest, treatment, reinvention, and the guidance of the Cardinals' trainer staff brought Wainwright back for reassuring appearances late in 2018. He scribbled on a napkin his proposed contract for a return in 2019 — and that was when renewed health, revised stuff, and that familiar confidence began to mesh and meet him on that drive to face the Sox.

In the first game of a doubleheader on Aug. 15, 2020, Wainwright pitched five innings and limited the stocked Sox to one run on two hits. He followed that start with consecutive seven-inning starts and then, on his 39th birthday, gave an overtaxed bullpen a gift with a complete-game shutout. Circumstances did in 2020 what injuries elsewhere in the rotation have in 2021 — thrust him into a leading role. He's responded by not just being the best pitcher on the staff, but one of the best in the league.

Since that pitstop in the rental car, Wainwright has made 35 starts — the equivalent of a full season. He's 17-10 with a 3.06 ERA. Those 17 wins lead the majors in the past year, his 229⅓ innings are second in the majors. Only two pitchers, Phillies' Zack Wheeler and Milwaukee's Brandon Woodruff, have more than 200 innings and a smaller ERA than Wainwright since Aug. 15, 2020. In the same month he turned 40, the oldest active National Leaguer, he also won the league's award for best pitcher, going 5-1 with a 1.43 ERA. In three of his previous four starts he hasn't allowed a run. It's been six weeks since he allowed more than three in a start. Seven years after he finished third for the award, Cy Young Award votes will await him after a strong September.

Tone set.

With health, he had the drive.

With Molina, he sees the destination.

"It's a special number. If we do get that number (325) I don't think anybody will ever break it," Wainwright said. "That's kind of one of the biggest thoughts that I have about coming back. Not only just winning — but that's like an all-time thing. How many people can say they have an all-time major-league record?" ∎

A WARM WELCOME

Teammates embrace the arrival of Molina

By Ben Frederickson
March 22, 2022

JUPITER, Fla. — This camp finally feels right.

The Cardinals' cornerstone catcher is back with his baseball flock.

Equipment bag slung over his shoulder, Raiders football hat atop his head, future Hall of Famer Yadier Molina walked up the sidewalk that leads from the Roger Dean Stadium players' parking lot, entered the clubhouse and emerged wearing Cardinals gear.

A celebration was underway.

Cardinals president of baseball operations John Mozeliak met Molina in the parking lot for a hug. Adam Wainwright's young son, Caleb, insisted his dad take him to see his baseball uncle. When clubhouse doors closed for a team meeting, a round of applause penetrated the wall.

Safe to assume it was the team welcoming back Molina after his report date was delayed by a week?

"Accurate," manager Oliver Marmol said with a grin.

Marmol was a Cardinals minor-league player when he first met Molina. The major-league catcher came to speak to the young guys. Now Marmol, 35, is the 39-year-old 10-time All-Star's manager.

Molina is both a constant and a catalyst. To say he was missed last week would be an understatement of massive proportions. The Cardinals aren't yet ready to think about Molina not being around. That's supposed to be a next-season story, after his retirement, not a surreal this-season feeling.

His absence made camp feel foreign. His arrival? As minor-league reliever James Naile, a product of Cape Girardeau, told new Cardinals starter Steven Matz, "He kind of turned a house into a home."

There are some concerns about how Molina's missed week and his impacted offseason could affect his performance this season, but two things felt miles ahead in importance Monday.

First, you hope everything is OK with Molina and his loved ones as the family works through the matter that kept the catcher in Puerto Rico until now. The team was informed of the delay after the MLB lockout ended.

Cardinals catcher Yadier Molina, right, hugs center fielder Harrison Bader after Molina reported Monday to the team's spring-training facility in Jupiter, Fla. It was the eighth day of camp.

Cardinals catcher Yadier Molina jumps off third base during a baserunning drill at spring training on Monday.

"I know it's going to be my last. I'm going to try to enjoy it. Keep working hard. Try to help the team win."

—Yadier Molina

"Personal reasons," is the phrase being used for now. If Molina chooses to share more eventually, that's up to him. But those close to him insist he is physically healthy and that this was a non-baseball situation.

"It's been tough, the last couple months," Molina said. "But everything is right, right now. I'm happy to be back."

Second, you could not help but notice how spirits lifted the second Molina made the hard left turn from the clubhouse door to his locker, where his uniform waited in anticipation.

His pitchers raced to offer fist-bumps and slaps on the back. His musical playlist was the one picked for backfield batting practice. His short meeting with reporters turned his corner of the clubhouse into a can of sardines, but no one minded, not even infielder Tommy Edman, who had no clear path to his own locker.

Molina said he's going to take things slow. Monday was supposed to be an in-and-out day. He wound up staying until the early evening after a grueling workout. When asked what happened to in-and-out, he grinned and offered a shrug. Good sign.

Molina's agent, Melvin Roman, reached out to the Cardinals after the lockout ended and players and owners could communicate again to let the team know about Molina's situation. The Cardinals told the catcher to take time. Fingers were crossed. Finally, a sigh of relief.

"We decided to figure out everything down in Puerto Rico, and that's what I did," Molina said. "Everything's good right now. I'm happy to be here."

And he's candid about what comes next.

Molina has been working out, he said, but he offered that he is not in his usual catching shape upon arrival. In the past, Molina arrives to spring slimmed down and gains some weight back as the season progresses. That schedule has been affected. Molina indicated he had not been taking live at-bats. He took multiple rounds Monday, not stopping until sweat dripped from the tip of his nose.

"It's probably going to take me four or five days to start playing games, to be able to be on the field again, just because I haven't seen pitches since last year," Molina said. "That's the tougher part."

Time will tell how fast Molina gets into catching shape and tunes up his timing at the plate. How much he plays in this final season and how opportunities are split between him and Andrew Knizner are sure to be topics of much discussion and debate.

Molina has some hard work ahead of him, but he's no stranger to that. If he was, he would not have reported to every Cardinals major-league camp since backup catcher Joe Girardi's side strain led to more spring-training reps for Molina in 2003, which resulted in manager Tony La Russa praising the 20-year-old non-roster invitee.

"He goes about playing the game right," La Russa told the Post-Dispatch 19 years ago this week, after Molina sprawled out near a dugout to catch a foul ball. "He's really something."

Still true.

"I know it's going to be my last," Molina said about this camp. "I'm going to try to enjoy it. Keep working hard. Try to help the team win."

On Monday, that was the big story. That Molina was back with his Cardinals, back to work for one last go. This was a day to celebrate. ■

MOLINA'S LARGESSE BETTER THAN A SHIRT OFF HIS BACK

By Ben Frederickson
March 25, 2022

JUPITER, Fla. — Ralph Scott Torrellas has a new suit story to tell.

As a wardrobe designer for some of baseball's biggest stars, the man players just refer to as, "Scott," uses his trusty tape measure and a discerning eye for prints to help famous athletes make fashion statements.

Torrellas, owner of Raphael Wardrobe Design, has a cellphone contact list that would make baseball agents drool. He has become a spring-training staple, making the rounds from camp to camp in Florida and Arizona to meet with players who are hungry for wardrobe upgrades. Usually his clients are buying for their own closets. Sometimes, they have someone else in mind. But Torrellas never has encountered an order quite like the one he just carried out of Cardinals camp.

"I don't think it's ever been done, and I've been doing this 30 years," Torrellas said.

This week behind the Cardinals clubhouse at Roger Dean Stadium, a table could be found covered with samples of high-end fabric. Rich colors and handsome textures fluttered in the breeze. If you're looking for something subtle, like a gray or blue suit, Torrellas has it. If you want to go loud, with bright splashes or a floral print, no problem. If you prefer to settle somewhere in between, a nice pinstripe, perhaps, he will gladly be your guide.

Torrellas is known here. Cardinals catcher Yadier Molina is one of his most loyal clients. The two were introduced by Albert Pujols years ago, back when Molina was just beginning his marathon run in the majors. Molina ordering something from Torrellas is nothing new. Neither is a player ordering a suit for a rookie or a favorite coach. Especially around here. The tradition is stitched into Cardinals baseball.

Manager Oliver Marmol, then the team's bench coach, was presented a jacket by then-manager Mike Shildt when they worked together. Second baseman Tommy Edman received a suit from his agent last season. Scott Rolen bought Adam Wainwright two suits early in his career.

"I still have them, too," Wainwright said. "I gave away all of the other old suits that don't fit or were styled different, but I kept those two, because those were my first two. It's something that is an important part of being a veteran leader in the clubhouse."

So, nothing was out of the ordinary when Molina asked Torrellas to measure beloved coach Jose Oquendo for a couple of suits the catcher wanted to give Oquendo as a gift. But then Molina pulled Torrellas aside and asked him if he could come back to camp for a second day. He did, and when he arrived there was a list waiting.

A steady wave of Cardinals employees soon started stopping by Torrellas' table. These were not his usual clients. Cardinals coaches made their way out to the patio, kicked off their shoes and stood statue-still for measurements. Then clubhouse workers started getting in line. They were filling out order forms, debating which patterns to pick, deciding if they wanted buttons or French cuffs, and letting Torrellas know if they wore a watch, and if so on which wrist, so he could leave a little extra room at the end of that sleeve. They were having a blast. Torrellas was getting a workout.

"Can someone bring me a Red Bull?" he asked at one point.

Pitching coach Mike Maddux got a little extra length in the leg because he wears cowboy boots. Bench coach Skip Schumaker noted he prefers understated colors. Willie McGee joked he probably wouldn't wear his nearly enough. "Thank you," longtime clubhouse attendant Patrick Cramer told Torrellas after he confirmed this will be his first custom-made suit.

"Don't thank me," Torrellas corrected with a smile. "Thank Yadi."

Yes, Molina had Torrellas size every member of the coaching and clubhouse staff for a suit. Everything uniquely made, down to the number of buttons. The list was 20 names, then grew longer. Molina kept adding to it, even sending over some coaches from the minor league side. The catcher, entering his 19th and final season with the only team he's ever known, is picking up the substantial tab.

"I've got to take care of my coaches," Molina said. "Simple reason. That's it."

That's Molina. Few words. Big actions. Before he starts this goodbye season, the future Hall of Famer is saying thanks.

"I can't remember the last time I measured that many people like that," Torrellas said. "It was kind of wild, spur of the moment. He thought it was a good idea. I told him when I thanked him, 'Do you know what's awesome about this gift? It's not like a vacation. It's not like a gift certificate to a fancy steakhouse, or a real expensive bottle of scotch. This is something that, every time they put this on, they're going to think of you.' They will own that thing the rest of their lives."

The gesture will last as long if not longer than the threads.

"Legend," Harrison Bader said. "Yadi always talks about how the Cardinals have helped him and have been a part of his life, and his family's life, for so long."

"He cares about people a ton," said Marmol. "He's always looking for opportunities to do stuff like that, especially when it's unexpected. The majority of time, nobody knows about it."

"The guy has a lot of love in him," added Wainwright. "He's got a lot of fight in him, too. But he's got a lot of love in him. Once you get into Yadi's inner circle, he will give you the shirt off his back."

Usually that's just a phrase. This time, it's a fact. Shirts will be included with the suits, thanks to the treasured catcher who decided to give a lasting gift.

"Nobody," Wainwright said, "Is going to get rid of those suits." ∎

Cardinals starting pitcher Adam Wainwright tips his cap to a standing ovation as he and catcher Yadier Molina take to the field for the 325th time as a major-league battery, breaking the record set in 1975 when Detroit's Mickey Lolich and Bill Freehan got to 324, during warmups before the first inning against the Brewers on Wednesday, Sept. 14, 2022, at Busch Stadium.

WAINWRIGHT, MOLINA EARN HISTORIC VICTORY

Cardinals' early power, late relief back battery

By Derrick Goold
September 15, 2022

The start made history.

The finish made them a winner.

And one late milestone stroke made Wednesday all the more memorable.

Adam Wainwright and Yadier Molina reset the major-league record for most starts as a tandem with the first pitch against the Milwaukee Brewers at Busch Stadium, their 325th together. What made them a winner was the work that followed. Staked to a lead by home runs from Nolan Arenado and Lars Nootbaar off Corbin Burnes, the reigning Cy Young Award winner, the Cardinals' bullpen worked four scoreless innings to reward the battery with a 4-1 victory in front of a sellout crowd of 46,459.

The Cardinals' final run of the evening, delivered in the bottom of the eighth, gave the evening additional gloss. Albert Pujols, in the lineup at designated hitter, doubled home the Cardinals' fourth run of the evening for the 2,200th RBI of his career. He joined Babe Ruth and Hank Aaron as the only three players in history with that many runs batted in.

The win restored the Cardinals' eight-game lead in the National League Central and with only two games remaining with the Brewers cleaved the magic number down to 12.

That countdown continues.

A count up that began a little more than five years ago reached what was once unsure — that two players, in their early 40s, would remain on the same team and together long enough to make 325 starts together. The number became a private quest for Wainwright and Molina, and a few people close to the catcher described this past week how sharing that major-league record with Wainwright was part of what drove Molina to return this season at age 40 and return from injury in the middle of this season.

The Cardinals' tandem, as close as brothers despite spending so much time 60 feet, 6 inches apart, broke a record held for generations by Detroit's Mickey Lolich and Bill Freehan. With each start they put the unreachable further ahead, as no other active battery is within 200 of them, and third on the list is Molina at (and) Jack Flaherty, at 69. Molina has three of the highest active totals.

For his third consecutive start, Wainwright (11-9) pitched five innings and nothing beyond. He yielded the mound and a two-run lead to the bullpen. Andre Pallante, Jordan Hicks, Giovanny Gallegos and Ryan Helsley carved through the next four innings to keep Milwaukee from mustering a challenge to that lead and play spoiler to the evening.

Helsley struck out two in the ninth to secure his 17th save.

HOME RUNS CARRY CARDINALS TO LEAD

It took two swings for the Cardinals to put a rally in gear to reclaim the lead for Wainwright shortly after he first misplaced it.

The Brewers, on a sacrifice fly, took a 1-0 lead in the top of the second. The first two batters of the bottom of the second inning struck with hits. Arenado led off the inning with his 29th home run of the season, tying the game. Brendan Donovan followed with a single. The inning ultimately found Molina with one out and runners at the corners. The Cardinals' catcher delivered the go-ahead RBI with a line-drive single to left.

A 2-1 lead meant Molina had the 31st go-ahead RBI of his career in a game started by Wainwright. That,

fittingly, tied him for the third most all-time. One of the other catchers he's tied with, fittingly, is Freehan, who also had 31 go-ahead RBIs in Lolich starts.

Three innings later, came a homer from one of the batters the Cardinals thought would be a strong matchup for them against pitchers like Burnes. Nootbaar connected on a 2-0 pitch and drove it 452 feet to center field. Nootbaar's 12th homer of the season widened the Cardinals lead for the bullpen to hold.

WAINWRIGHT SIDESTEPS TROUBLE, TWICE

In each of his previous two starts, Wainwright felt like his delivery was out of sync, and the line scores reflected how he felt.

He allowed four runs on nine hits in five innings each game, and after the second one — a loss to Washington — he described the work that he had to do in the bullpen. Cardinals manager Oliver Marmol attended part of the bullpen to see the right-hander work, listening as he stopped after each pitch to adjust what he felt was oft-kilter, what stretch of his leg or shift of his torso was throwing off the timing and then the movement of his pitches.

"He hasn't been good the last two times out, and he hasn't looked right," Marmol said. "But the work that goes into the bullpen and figuring out why is my body is not in sync, why are my pitches not doing what they're supposed to do — when you're as confident as he is in his abilities (the work is clear). There's this back and forth collaboration after each pitch in figuring out and he'll figure it out. That's what he's done his whole career."

He did but not for the whole of his start Wednesday.

Christian Yelich showed no intention of swinging at the first pitch as Wainwright and Molina assured the record-setting start. He let history happen.

The former MVP saw two more pitches before striking out on a called strike three. The inning went sideways from there. Two singles and a two-out walk loaded the bases on Wainwright and brought Andrew McCutchen to the plate. Another former MVP — and

St. Louis Cardinals pitcher Adam Wainwright and catcher Yadier Molina talk in the dugout during the fifth inning against the Atlanta Braves on Sunday, Aug. 28, 2022, at Busch Stadium.

the one who has faced Wainwright the most often in his career — McCutchen gave Wainwright a gift. An excuse-me swing with a bouncer back to the pitcher to strand three runners.

It was the first of two times in the first four innings that Milwaukee would leave the bases loaded.

The second began with back-to-back singles and a sacrifice fly that gave Milwaukee the first lead of the game. Before Wainwright could regain control of the inning, the Brewers had three singles and the run in. But the rally wheezed from there. In the fourth, the bottom of the Brewers' order again sparked a threat. With two outs, Milwaukee got two singles and a walk from Wainwright to load the bases. The inning ended with a fly out.

Through four innings, Wainwright had bobbed and weaved and curved his way out of trouble — and the Brewers had left eight runners on base, five in scoring position.

A SIGNATURE DOUBLE PLAY

An escape from one inning had all the feel of Pearl Jam playing "Alive" or Wainwright warming up to Blake Shelton's "God's Country" — a reliable show playing the classic.

With former teammate Kolten Wong at first and one out, Wainwright once again faced McCutchen. No active player has more than McCutchen's 84 plate appearances against Wainwright, and no active player has more than McCutchen's 17 strikeouts in those plate appearances. Wainwright could not land his cutter for a strike against the veteran designated hitter. He got the first strike of the at-bat when McCutchen clipped a sinker for a foul ball. Wainwright slipped a curve past McCutchen before the cutter again failed to nick the strike zone.

With a 3-2 count, Wainwright went back to his is trusty and true curve.

The 74-mph bender dipped past McCutchen's swing for a strikeout, and Molina provided the chef's kiss. He backhanded the pitch while getting to his feet for a throw to second. Wainwright's signature pitch would be turned into Molina's signature play. The catcher's strike beat Wong by a stride for strikeout/throw-out double play that ended the inning.

Molina wagged his finger, slightly. ∎

A BIG SEND-OFF

FOR PUJOLS, MOLINA; WAINO STRUGGLES

Marmol brings the three Cardinals stars off the field together

By Rick Hummel
Monday, October 3, 2022

When Cardinals manager Oliver Marmol came to the mound with two outs in the fifth inning Sunday and the Cardinals down 6-5, Adam Wainwright knew he was done. He didn't know that his longtime catcher and first baseman were going to walk to the dugout with him.

"That was a surprise," Wainwright said. "I thought that was cool."

But he added, "I was done. I needed to be done."

Cardinals veterans Yadier Molina, left, Adam Wainwright, center, and Albert Pujols leave the field on Sunday, Oct. 2, 2022, after being removed in the fifth inning of a game against the Pirates at Busch Stadium. Pujols and Molina, who have announced plans to retire at season's end, were honored in ceremonies before what was their final home regular-season contest.

Wainwright, who hasn't announced any retirement plans as have Yadier Molina and Albert Pujols, allowed six hits and four runs in 4⅔ innings of the Cardinals' 7-5 loss to the Pittsburgh Pirates. Some were bloops. But a leadoff walk bedeviled him in the second, as did a Ben Gamel three-run homer off a bad sinker.

The plan had been for Wainwright, who has one win in exactly a month, to throw 50 or so pitches, "get on track and get out of there," he said.

But he ended up throwing 86 pitches, 53 for strikes.

"I was proud to walk off the field with those guys even though I was pouting a little bit," he said. "It still was a good moment for me to say I was teammates with two of the greatest ever. That was a cool time for Albert and Yadi and our whole team to see how St. Louis celebrates some of the greatest players, not just Cardinals, but players ever."

Molina said he had been hoping to finish the fifth inning.

"Not everything is perfect," he said. "The moment was great just to walk with Albert and 'Waino' next to me. It was a great moment for baseball, I think."

Marmol, saying, "It was meaningful for all three of them to walk off at the same time," later said he probably should have made the move involving Wainwright and the other two an inning before that — after the right-hander had retired the first two hitters.

"I should have done it the other way," Marmol admitted.

Pujols, who would have led off the fifth, had homered in his second at-bat. That was in the third inning, when he lined No. 702 into the center-field greenery, and came after he had doubled home two runs in the first. Those three RBIs tied Pujols with Babe Ruth for second all-time, at 2,214, behind only Henry Aaron's 2,297.

"He always rises to the occasion in big moments," Wainwright said.

Marmol said he didn't want Pujols' next at-bat to take anything away from the home run he had just hit.

"Letting that be the last one for the regular season (at home) is not a bad way to go out," Marmol said. "He continues to 'wow' everybody."

Marmol could have pinch-hit for Pujols in the fifth but would have found that awkward. And he didn't want Wainwright to finish with a losing record and if he could make it through the fifth, he could have a winning record.

Pujols didn't bat again.

"We have more games to play so it's not like it's our last game," Pujols said. "I know 'Waino' can be a little disappointed. He wished he would have got the win and pitched better, but not everything can go perfect. At the end of the day I think it's really exciting. Three more games left in the regular season and get ready for the postseason."

Wainwright did end up with a losing record (11-12) and, having given up 44 hits and 23 runs in his past 28⅔ innings over six starts, is in trouble for making the postseason roster.

Maybe even the end of his career looms larger. Someone close to Wainwright thought that a month ago, when Wainwright had a 3.09 ERA, that it was fairly certain the 41-year-old would be back. Now, no one really is sure.

Wainwright's face while he was sitting in the dugout, showed his frustration.

"Yeah, I'm frustrated. I went from ... no doubt pitching Game 1 (of the team's opening-round playoff series) to maybe not pitching at all," he said. "I cannot control that. All I can do is keep making improvements.

"Breaking ball was better today. Cutter was much better today. Still got to work on my heater a little bit, looking to get a little more zip to that pitch. Timing of my delivery was still a little bit off."

But Wainwright had a handful of swings and misses, something he hadn't been doing with any pitch. "The velo(city) on the other two pitches (curveball and cutter) were back to where they needed to be," he said.

"Baby steps."

Marmol noted the improvement in Wainwright's pitches other than his fastball but added, "At the end of the day, you look at the (pitching) line and that's not what you want."

Ordinarily, Wainwright would not undertake participating in a pregame ceremony on the day he was pitching. But this was Yadi and Albert.

"I declined at first because I knew it was going to be in my warmup," he said. "And I was asked again. And I thought, you know what, this is a special time for those two and I feel like I owe it to them to be a part of it. I wouldn't have done it if I was a second-year player. But I've been here a long time and been teammates with them a long time and felt like I ought to. I wouldn't miss that."

Marmol said Wainwright could have filmed his remarks a day earlier.

"He could have done it a lot of different ways but he wanted to make sure it was special for those two guys," Marmol said.

Wainwright and Molina, who made their big-league record-extending 328th start together, have a special bond.

"I reminded Yadi the other day that he had set the record for most putouts (by a catcher). I got a bunch of those. He's welcome," said Wainwright, with as much of a joke as he could muster Sunday.

He normally takes little time in warming up but he said he didn't shortchange his prep work Sunday, so there was no excuse.

"We started late because I wasn't going to," he said.

But, after a five-pitch first inning, it went mostly downhill.

"This is bad timing," Wainwright said. "Every time you play a big-league season you're going to have a little series of games where things are not going your way. It's unfortunate this is the last month of the season. The only difference between this year and last year was my September was great last year, and this year it wasn't.

"I kind of ruined a good season with these last four starts. That's the first losing season I've ever had pitching a full season. Didn't get to 200 innings (191⅔) Didn't get to 200 wins (195). Didn't really do a dad-gum thing that I wanted to, except help us win some games.

"I also know I should have won a lot of games in the middle there when I pitched very well and

Yadier Molina and Adam Wainwright walk in from the bullpen before the start of a game between the Pirates and Cardinals at Busch Stadium on Sunday, Oct. 2, 2022.

didn't get any breaks. Yeah, just a tough ending. Good thing we've got another month to play."

Will we see him pitch again next weekend?

"I have no idea," Wainwright said. "I'm good enough to keep making adjustments and keep growing and gaining steam towards the end goal."

Miles Mikolas, the new staff ace, said, "He's gearing up for the playoffs and I'm sure he's got an extra playoff gear that a lot of people probably don't realize that he has. We know he'll be ready."

Pujols, who has a daughter with Down syndrome, historically had performed well on 'Buddy Walk' Day, once hitting three homers in one of those Sunday games here during his first tour with the Cardinals.

It was 'Buddy Walk Day' for Down syndrome kids at Busch Stadium on Sunday and Pujols didn't disappoint. After he left the game, Juan Yepez came in to play first base and had two doubles, giving the pair three doubles and a homer.

"Pretty good, huh?" Yepez said. "The Hall of Fame — and the future." ∎

POOF! CARDINALS' 'MAGIC' SEASON VANISHES IN SWEEP. THEIR NEXT TRICK IS UP TO NEW CORE

By Derrick Goold
October 9, 2022

As he walked to the plate with a chance to push the game one hit deeper into the night, the season one game further into the weekend, and his career one day longer into October, Yadier Molina paused and whispered a prayer.

He refused to be the last out of his last game.

"I was concentrating to not be," he said.

A 19-year career spent entirely with one organization and annually chasing one trophy, Molina stepped into the batter's box with two outs in the ninth inning Saturday night at Busch Stadium. He did then what he had done more than any player in National League history — delivered a base hit in the playoffs, for the 102nd time.

With the final swings of their major-league careers, Molina and Albert Pujols delivered singles and then yielded first base to a pinch-runner. They were in the dugout when the Cardinals' season unceremoniously ended in the glove of a former teammate, the Phillies' Edmundo Sosa, securing a 2-0 victory Saturday and a sweep in the wild-card series at Busch Stadium.

At 10:54 p.m. St. Louis time, it was sundown on a Cardinals era.

Careers that spanned a combined 41 seasons, 20 All-Star appearances, 12 Gold Glove awards and 5,498 games — including 194 in the postseason — ended in the blink of 18 innings.

The long goodbye had the shortest ending.

"It's the end of the Pujols-Molina era," Cardinals chairman Bill DeWitt Jr. said, walking into the clubhouse after the loss. "It's been a nice winning era, that's for sure."

"You're just expecting the story to continue, to be what it's always been," manager Oliver Marmol said.

"It wasn't meant to be for us this year," Pujols said.

EMOTIONAL SCENE

In the clubhouse after the loss, players exchanged hugs. Some packed their gear. Several players, such as Nolan Arenado, were on the verge of tears or coming back from taking the plunge.

St. Louis Cardinals catcher Yadier Molina hits a single with two outs in the bottom of the ninth with a man on base during Game 2 of the National League wild card series between the Philadelphia Phillies and St. Louis Cardinals at Busch Stadium in St. Louis on Saturday, Oct. 8, 2022. This was the last at-bat of Molina's career, he was pulled from the game for pinch runner after getting the hit.

Molina's voice snagged when describing the ovation he received from fans as he left the field for the final time. He shared a moment with backup catcher Andrew Knizner, just as rookie Juan Yepez walked with Pujols as he left the clubhouse as a player for the final time. The transition from one generation — one with two championships, Molina's four pennants, and 15 consecutive winning seasons — to the next, newer Cardinals core was underway.

Two immediate questions will start to shape it.

A potential face of the franchise for this next era of Cardinals, Arenado enjoyed his first division title in his second year in St. Louis. He has an opt-out clause in his contract and can become a free agent in four weeks. Or, he can remain a Cardinal through at least 2026. His choice. There is the possibility of negotiating a deal that at least guarantees the club option for 2027. Arenado, 31, repeatedly has said he intends to remain with the Cardinals, that he relishes the atmosphere at the ballpark, and he affirmed that again Saturday.

"I love it here. I love the guys. I feel like I fit well with this organization," Arenado said, pausing at times before tearing up. "I just feel like I fit well here. I think the city appreciates me. Probably not after tonight. I really loved it here. Hopefully we can figure it out."

Adam Wainwright, a 17-year veteran and third member of the advertised "last run," has yet to announce whether he will return for 2023 or retire. The Cardinals are open to another one-year deal with the right-hander. But his view of Molina's base hit will play into the decision.

Wainwright, 41, watched from the bullpen and saw a gap opening in right-center, nudging a longtime colleague that Molina was about to land a single right there. He'd seen him do it so often —just usually from the dugout. On the roster but not part of the rotation because of his difficulties in September, Wainwright said the vantage point of the bullpen is one "I don't like as much." It will be part of the conversation he has with family about one more year.

"We should know pretty soon if something happens," Wainwright said. "If not, then it's been a good run. Thanks, St. Louis. I don't like not pitching in a playoff series. So, you can take that one of two ways. You could take that as it's been a good run. Or, you could take that as a motivation to never let that happen again."

He said later he has his answer.

He did not divulge it, not yet.

The Cardinals went through the two games against Philadelphia without their last two pitchers to receive Cy Young Award votes throwing a single pitch. Jack Flaherty warmed up. Wainwright said he was ready to close, when needed. The Cardinals engaged the bullpen quickly Saturday, calling on lefty Jordan Montgomery to replace Miles Mikolas with two on in the fifth. Mikolas conceded the matchup of left-handed batters was better at that point for Montgomery and felt as he left the mound, "alright, here we go — punchout, pop out."

Montgomery allowed a sacrifice fly that doubled the Phillies' lead initially provided by Bryce Harper's solo homer of Mikolas. The scoreboard said the Cardinals trailed by two runs.

The gap did not feel that close.

It felt cavernous.

'WE DIDN'T HIT'

"We didn't hit the ball," Molina said bluntly.

"It got cold at the wrong time," Marmol said.

That has become the Cardinals' yearly forecast for October — a chill shivering through the lineup. The Cardinals are 1-9 in their last 10 playoff games, and they've been held to a run or less in six of those nine losses. Since the start of the 2019 National League Championship Series, the Cardinals have hit 33 for 220 (.150) in their past seven postseason games outside of 2020's bubble.

The Cardinals had one extra-base hit in Philly's two-day visit. The only runs the Cardinals' scored were provided on pinch-hits by rookies, Yepez and Nolan Gorman. The starters in the lineup combined to go 10 for 62 (.161). The Phillies' two starters, Zack Wheeler (Game 1) and Aaron Nola (Game 2), threw 13 scoreless innings. Nola did so by short-circuiting the middle of the Cardinals' order at the two MVP candidates who reside there, Paul Goldschmidt and Arenado.

In the sixth inning Saturday, Pujols lashed a one-out single to get the tying run to the plate.

Nola struck out Goldschmidt on six pitches.

He struck out Arenado on five pitches.

Goldschmidt and Arenado had six at-bats combined with a runner on base Saturday and went 0 for six with five strikeouts.

'I DIDN'T DO MY JOB'

"The results speak for themselves," Goldschmidt said. "I've played all September, now October, so it really stinks you know. And it's 100% on me. I didn't do my job and it stinks. I can't change it. I hate that. I think we're going to need some time to heal from this."

"I think we didn't come through," Arenado said. "I had opportunities to do it, and I didn't. I wouldn't have it any other way, right? I would rather be here talking to you guys than at home watching on the TV. It's unfortunate to lose the way we did."

In the eighth Saturday, there was one more chance for Arenado and Goldschmidt to turn over a new autumn leaf, to provide in the season's final month

Molina walked off, lowering his head as an ovation escorted him to the dugout. He stood not too far from Pujols for the final moments of their career.

what they did so often in the first six. It began with Pujols. The three-time MVP — in what would be his final major-league at-bat — greeted reliever Seranthony Dominguez with a single down the third-base line to get the tying run on base. Pujols was lifted for a pinch-runner, leaving the Busch Stadium field for the last time. Dominguez then struck out Goldschmidt and Arenado to end the inning.

In the ninth, Phillies closer Zach Elfin retired the first two batters he faced before Corey Dickerson's single gave Molina that last chance for his first hit of the series.

He flipped a single to right, right in the direction of Wainwright.

A pinch-runner trotted out and Molina walked off, lowering his head as an ovation escorted him to the dugout. He stood not too far from Pujols for the final moments of their career. The end came one batter later when Tommy Edman popped up.

Molina was asked in the clubhouse how he felt about a final day as Pujols' teammate.

"Albert?" Molina said. "I'm going to be his brother forever. Can't ask for more."

"We're so blessed," Pujols said. "We had unbelievable careers. I think we left a mark in every place."

There are two that hung above both of them as they spoke — the banners in the Cardinals' clubhouse for the 2006 and 2011 World Series championships. In the coming years there will be two more. Molina's No. 4 and Pujols' No. 5 will be retired by the team and hung alongside No. 6, No. 1, No. 2, Nos.17, 10, 6,

14, 24, 42, 20, and 45. Pujols motioned around that clubhouse late Saturday and noted the young talent that will continue to "make this team a contender."

THE NEXT CHAPTER

His season, often described as "magic" or "storybook," came to its conclusion, but as that chapter ends, the next for the Cardinals already has begun. The team traded for Goldschmidt and Arenado to be the next core, the one that carried the team for so much of this season and is expected to carry it into the next several and, by shaking their postseason blahs, reverse the trend of Cardinals' sudden exits.

Perhaps even be driven by them.

"That's exciting — you have two guys who are absolute pros, who invest in the younger group just like the guys before them did, and who find value in that," Marmol said, sitting in his office between visits from players for hugs. "They're not selfish. They understand that setting the culture is important, being held accountable is important, and holding others accountable is important. It's in good hands."

Producing in October is also important.

Molina and Pujols did until the very end.

That too is expected of Cardinals in any era, a reporter mentioned to the manager.

"That's why I used the word 'accountable,'" he said. "Those are still the guys I want up in the tough situations. I will count on them every time. The game (stinks). It punches you in the gut often but the moments that don't (stink) are really darn cool, and those keep you coming back." ■